Martin Bucer's Ground and Reason

A Commentary and Translation

by

Ottomar Frederick Cypris

Good Samaritan Books
Keeping hope and healing in Jesus Christ

Martin Bucer's Ground and Reason: A Commentary and Translation
Copyright © 2016 Christopher W. Bogosh. Permission was granted by the Cypris family to format, reproduce, and edit the work Ottomar Frederick Cypris for this present volume. The Cypris family possesses the copyright for the original manuscripts.

All rights reserved. No part of this book may be reproduced, stored in a retrieval system, or transmitted in any form by any means, electronic, mechanical, photocopy, recording, or otherwise, without the prior permission of Christopher W. Bogosh, except as provided by USA copyright law.

Good Samaritan Books
86395 Riverwood Drive
Yulee, FL 32097
chrisbogosh@gmail.com

Printed in the United States of America
ISBN-13: 978-1540468116
ISBN-10: 1540468119

Foreword by Dr. Glen J. Clary

As a result of his tireless quest for church unity, Martin Bucer has been called *the ecumenical Reformer*. Unfortunately, most of his efforts at achieving unity ended in failure. Though primarily remembered for his attempts to unify the church, Bucer's greatest contribution to the Reformation was not in the field of ecumenicity but in worship. According to Hughes Oliphant Old, "Among the Protestant Reformers of the sixteenth century, Martin Bucer had the most penetrating insight into the questions of the reform of worship"; moreover, "Bucer's work on the development of Protestant worship was without doubt his primary achievement."[1] Because of his pioneering endeavor to reform the worship of the church, Bucer deserves to be known as *the father of Reformed worship*.

In 1524, Bucer and his colleagues in the city of Strasbourg began implementing various changes in the church's liturgy. By the end of that year, a German baptismal service had been published. The Mass had not yet been abolished, but many priests had started administering an evangelical form of the Lord's Supper. Protestant ministers had openly denounced numerous man-made ceremonies and liturgical traditions that were not sanctioned by the Word of God. These efforts to revise the liturgy were motivated by a desire to worship the Lord according to Scripture and the customs of the ancient church. Such worship, they argued, was the only worship acceptable to God and beneficial for His people.

On behalf of the Reformed ministers of Strasbourg, Bucer wrote a defense of their liturgical reforms entitled *Grund und Ursach* (Ground and Reason), which first appeared on the day after Christmas in 1524. This bold and lively defense of the Reformation "is one of the most significant documents in the history of Reformed worship."[2] It provides a clear window through

---

[1] Hughes Oliphant Old, *The Reading and Preaching of the Scriptures in the Worship of the Christian Church*, vol. 4 (Grand Rapids, MI: Eerdmans, 2002) 72, 74.
[2] Hughes Oliphant Old, *Worship: Reformed According to Scripture*, Revised and Expanded

which one can see how liturgical revisions were introduced, explained, and defended in one of the major centers of the Reformation in the first half of the sixteenth century. In this early apology of Reformed worship, we discover how the first Reformers, when Protestant theology was still in its germinal stage, attempted to recover the worship practices of the apostolic age. Seven of the eleven chapters are dedicated to the subject of the Lord's Supper. At the time of its writing, Bucer's doctrine of the Eucharist was heavily influenced by Zwingli, but his desire to unite the Zwinglians and Lutherans would soon lead him to pursue a mediating position, which position later influenced John Calvin and, through him, most of the Reformed world. In *Grund und Ursach*, we discover the Reformed doctrine and practice of the Lord's Supper and other liturgical ordinances in their nascent form.

In 2017, which marks the 500th anniversary of Protestantism, we remember and celebrate the important events that started the Reformation, such as Martin Luther nailing his Ninety-five Theses to the church door on October 31, 1517. One of the most important events that should be remembered and commemorated in our celebration is the introduction of Reformed worship in the city of Strasbourg, which Bucer describes and defends in this seminal treatise. Brian Nicholson is to be commended for his excellent and valuable work in making *Grund und Ursach* available to English readers just in time for the celebration.

Dr. Glen J. Clary
December 14, 2016

Edition (Louisville, KY: Westminster John Knox Press, 2002) 12.

Preface by Rev. Brian Nicholson

For many years, to read Martin Bucer's *Grund und Ursach* in English, it was necessary to secure a physical copy of Dr. Ottomar Cypris's dissertation manuscript from someone who owned a copy or to purchase the dissertation in PDF form from University Microfilms, Inc. of Ann Arbor Michigan. German readers could of course read Bucer's *Deutsche Schriften* published by Gütersloher Verlagshaus. Recently, images of the entire first edition of *Grund* have been made available online by the Bayerische StaatsBibiliothek.[3]

When Dr. Terry Johnson, senior minister of Independent Presbyterian Church in Savannah, Georgia, told me about Bucer's book on worship, I asked him where I could get a copy. Dr. Johnson graciously loaned me a copy of Dr. Cypris's dissertation which included a German to English translation. Having read it and recognizing its importance, I posed the question to Dr. Johnson, "Why isn't this in print?" His response to me was unexpected, "Perhaps you could publish it." That word of encouragement launched a sixteen year-long project.

It was first necessary to locate the family of the late Dr. Cypris in order to secure permission to publish their father's work. Using the internet, Mr. Darcy Cypris was not difficult to locate in British Columbia. Mr. Cypris enthusiastically granted the necessary permission to proceed.

Next I needed to find a publisher. Three publishing houses specializing in Reformation literature came to mind. Over the next two years, all three publishers turned down the project. Then, in the year 2010, I met Mr. Ivan Rocha who began attending my church in Medford, Oregon. Ivan became interested in the project and we spoke about using an online self-publishing approach to get the work in print. We purchased a copy of the dissertation in PDF from Proquest Publishing Company (formerly University Microfilms) and, using OCR software, Ivan transformed the manuscript into ed-

---

[3] See http://reader.digitale-sammlungen.de/resolve/display/bsb10167779.html.

itable form and the two of us worked through *Grund* and Dr. Cypris's *Commentary*, correcting the errata that the OCR software inevitably introduced into the text and also updating Dr. Cypris's typewritten format. When Ivan and his family moved to Ohio, our project ground to a halt. The files remained on my computer.

Mr. Christopher Bogosh, a book author and publisher, arrived in Medford in 2015 and began attending my church. When Chris learned about my passion to see Bucer's work in print, he too took up the cause and with great determination formatted the files into book form to be published under the imprint of Good Samaritan Books. Dr. Martin Emmrich of Corvallis, Oregon translated one untranslated German paragraph in the text of the *Commentary*. Dr. Glen Clary contributed a Foreword to the work. We are all together gratified that this project—Dr. Ottomar Cypris's marvelous English translation of and his commentary on Martin Bucer's *Grund und Ursach*— can now finally be presented to students of Reformation history, theology and worship.

Soli Deo Gloria

Rev. Brian Nicholson
December 2016

Biographical Sketch of Ottomar Frederick Cypris

Ottomar was born in Ohra, a suburb of the Free City of Danzig,[4] on May 2, 1915. At age fifteen, while attending the Oberrealschule of Danzig,[5] Cypris immigrated to Canada and lived with relatives in the city of Edmonton, Alberta, where he went to high school at King Edward Junior High. In 1935 Ottomar enrolled in the University of Alberta. He graduated with a Bachelor of Arts degree in 1938 and matriculated a Masters of Arts in 1941. His thesis was "*Heinrich Heine als Ritter des Heiligen Geistes.*"[6] During these years, Ottomar was awarded a teaching fellowship for German in the Department of Modern Languages at the University of Alberta.

In 1938, Cypris entered St. Stephen's College, a divinity school associated with the United Church of Canada, where he received ordination in 1942 at Edmonton, Alberta. Before relocating to New York City to study at Union Theological Seminary, Ottomar served two pastorates in the Alberta Conference, Alliance Hopefield (1942–1947) and Calgary (1947–1951). During his final year at Calgary, Ottomar was awarded a Bible Doctorate in the field of New Testament Worship.

After arriving in New York, Cypris entered Union Theological Seminary with the intention of becoming a professor of Homiletics and Liturgics, until he came into contact with Dr. John T. McNeill and Dr. C. C. Richardson. Underneath their tutelage, guidance, and inspiration he was set on a course of study in Reformed and Protestant worship. His Master's Thesis in 1953 was on "Public Worship in Calvin," which was written in partial fulfillment his of Master of Sacred Theology Degree which was awarded in 1953. His

---

[4] The location of this city is in modern day Poland to the north, on the coast of the Baltic Sea.
[5] This is a secondary school in Danzig that focuses on science and mathematics.
[6] "Heinrich Heine as a Knight of the Holy Spirit" is the translation from German. Christian Johann Heinrich Heine (1797–1856) was a German writer known for his lyric poetry, satire, and literary criticism.

magnum opus was Martin Bucer's *Grund und Ursach* (Ground and Reason), which was completed in May of 1971.

Aside from his theological acumen, experience in liturgics, and capability as a pastor; Cypris was also fluent in German. At least to my knowledge, there were no documents by the Strasbourg Reformers translated from German into English in the 1970s. All of these factors, not to mention Cypris's expert guidance by McNeill and Richardson converged to form a perfect storm. The result was one of the earliest documents of Reformed and Protestant worship available to the English reader. The late Oliphant Hughes Old hailed *Grund und Ursach* as "one of the most significant documents in the history of Reformed worship."[7]

Cypris's completed *Grund und Ursach* while serving his professorship at the University of West Virginia which began in the fall of 1969, and gave these heartfelt comments concerning his life's work:

> I came to West Virginia University as my field of future activity, teaching in the field of the History of Christian Thought, because making some contribution to the academic life in an underprivileged state not only affords me the opportunity to repay a debt to all my good teachers…in Western Canada but especially at Union Theological Seminary.

This bears the heart of a true pastor who is always seeking to pass on the Faith. In addition to extensive pastoral work, Ottomar also held academic positions at Mount Royal College, Calgary, Alberta, teaching German; Union Theological Seminary, as an Assistant Director for Field Work; Assistant Professor in the Department of Religion at Lehigh University, Bethlehem, Pennsylvania; and as Adjunct Professor at Rutgers University, New Brunswick, New Jersey.

In July of 1986, Dr. Cypris joined the saints and Jesus in Paradise.

---

[7] Old, *Worship*, 12.

Author's Preface

Martin Bucer's *Grund und Ursach*, described by Julius Smend as the most important liturgical writing produced in the era of the Reformation, was published in Strassburg on December 26, 1524. Bucer and eight other Strassburg Reformers co-signed the document.

The covering letter which precedes *Grund und Ursach* is addressed to Duke Frederick, Count Palatine, whom Bucer had served as chaplain for a year. In it Bucer justifies on scriptural grounds the reforms accomplished in Strassburg. He also attacks the spiritual leaders of the Church for their anti-Christian, immoral lives; for having condemned and persecuted the evangelical leaders without a proper trial; for encouraging the abuses in the Church; and for exploiting the superstitions of the common people for their own gain. He insists that the Strassburg preachers are ruled by the Word of God and that they do obey the regularly constituted civil authorities. He defends himself and the other Reformers against the calumnies of their opponents.

Grund und Ursach gives scriptural authority for the reforms undertaken in Strassburg. The basic principles which underlie this "return to that which is old and eternal" are an absolute acceptance of the Word of God as rule and norm: everything contrary to the Word of God must be and has been abolished, and further, their pairing of faith and love. Faith is acceptance of the saving, once-for-all death of Christ. For the sake of love for the weaker brethren, all innovations must be introduced slowly and gently, as the end result of faithful teaching and preaching by the Reformers. Through the death of Christ, Christian freedom has been won for all who believe and all external forms of worship are empty unless they express reality in worship. These basic elements are applied by Bucer to his doctrine of the sacraments and to the liturgy.

The Lord's Supper is not a sacrifice but rather a sign and a symbol. Its effectiveness lies in the hearts of those who, with faith in the once-for-all death of Christ, eat His flesh and drink His blood spiritually. Other important aspects of the Lord's Supper which Bucer emphasizes are *anamnesis*, *eucharistia* and *synaxis*.

Grund und Ursach reflects Bucer's shift from the "Lutheran" to the "Zwinglian" position, retaining, however, some characteristic emphases of each. The shift was caused by several factors: first, the confusion among the Strassburg populace, and the uncertainty and indecision of the Strassburg preachers, brought about by the presence, activity, teaching and writings of Carlstadt; second, Hoen's letter suggesting that *est* in the words of institution means *significat*; third, Zwingli, whose teaching and whose example in the introduction of the Reformation in Zurich became Bucer's model.

Grund und Ursach spells out the application of the basic principles to the liturgical reforms. The radical simplicity of the Reformed worship in Strassburg was modified by the introduction of congregational signing. From the very first fixed forms of worship were provided. These, through Calvin, became influential in the later development of Reformed worship.

Grund und Ursach is historically important because it is a prototype of the manner in which the Reformation was introduced in other German cities, and also because it was produced in Strassburg, where the sacramental controversies, which were to divide European Protestantism, had their beginning.

MARTIN BUCER'S GROUND AND REASON

A COMMENTARY

BY

OTTOMAR FREDERICK CYPRIS

Introduction

When Bucer arrived in Strassburg as an exile on May 18, 1523, he had no idea that twenty-six years later he would leave Strassburg as an exile, in April 1549. There was this difference, however, that when he left Strassburg,[1] he was no longer an unknown ex-monk, recently married, appealing for the protection of an important German city government, but a highly respected reformer whose genius for union efforts was widely recognized and who had left his mark on the religious life of Europe. When leaving Strassburg he received invitations to take refuge in Wittenberg, Bern, Geneva, Copenhagen and England. It was in England, revered as a reformer and respected as a professor at Cambridge University, that he spent the remainder of his life—less than two years. He died on February 28, 1551, and was buried with the highest honors.

It was the tragedy of Bucer's life that in all those concerns which were of vital importance to him he was either a complete or a qualified failure. It had been one of the great dreams of his life to create a union of church and state in which the church was to be of equal or even superior importance in matters of organization, teaching and discipline. He succeeded partially in one but failed in the other because the *Rat*[2] of Strassburg, unwilling to repeat an early domination of the city by the Roman Catholic Church, this time by Protestant domination, prevented its realization.

The other great aspiration of his life was to unite a Protestantism torn apart by sacramental controversies. It had become his great, magnificent obsession; he sped o'er land and sea, sacrificed his own comfort and that of his family, was misunderstood by his friends and abused by his enemies, but could not be turned aside from that purpose. "My aim is, although I

---

[1] Editor's footnote: "Strassburg" and "Strasbourg" are used interchangeably.
[2] *Rat* here used for *Magistrat*. Since the English translation is misleading as to the function of this law-making body in Strassburg the German term *Rat* will be used throughout. For the best treatment *cf. Magistrat und Reformation* in Strassburg bis 1529 by Adolf Baum, Strassburg, 1887.

pursue it not always with the necessary warmth and broadmindedness, that Christians should recognize and embrace each other in love; for all defects in customs and judgment result from the fact that, because of weak concord, the spirit of Christ misses its effect…"[3] The Marburg Colloquy of 1529 was only partially successful[4] in uniting the Lutherans and Zwinglians; the best that the Wittenberg Concord of 1536[5] achieved was the union of the Lutherans and the south German churches and a temporary peaceful coexistence with all of the Zwinglians, who were destined to go their separate ways in the end.

Like many peacemakers and representatives of the via media, he was distrusted by one side, as in the case of Luther, and hated by the other, as in the case of Bullinger. To a great extent Bucer himself was responsible for these attitudes. His well-meant tactics were not only over-eager, but even questionable at times. His constant search for uniting formulae only too often could be interpreted in terms of superficiality or duplicity. The same terms or phrases used by opposing parties were often interpreted in quite different and divergent ways. This aspect of Bucer's activity was clearly recognized by Calvin when, writing to Farel from the *Reichstag* of Regensburg on May 12, 1541, he stated: "Philip and Bucer have drawn up ambiguous and insincere formulas concerning transubstantiation, to try whether they could satisfy the opposite party by yielding nothing."[6] Calvin goes on to say that he disapproves of this device because, in their methods, "they accommodate themselves too much to the time. But I cannot well endure to see that Bucer so loads himself with the hatred of many on account of it." With deep insight into Bucer's real motives, he admits that "both are animated with the best intentions and have no other object in view than promoting the kingdom of Christ."

The hope of uniting Protestants and Catholics was shattered at the con-

---

[3] T. Schiess, *Briefwechsel der Gebruder Blaurer*, Freiburg, 1910, I, p.742.
[4] It was a partial success, because in 1530, at Augsburg, three confessions were submitted, *Cf.* p.21, below, also John T. McNeill. *Unitive Protestantism*, Richmond, 1964, p.144.
[5] *Ibid.*, pp.152-162.
[6] *Letters of John Calvin.* Jules Bonnet. Vol. l, p. 239. Edinburgh, 1855

ferences of Hagenau, Worms and Regensburg[7] when, in spite of willingness to make concessions, a point was reached when to compromise any further Protestant principles meant that Protestantism itself would disappear. This was also true at the Interim negotiations,[8] when the Emperor tried to use Bucer's well-known mediating and conciliating attitudes and his recognized skill, to further his own political ends. Bucer, defying the Emperor, secretly fled from Augsburg and in turn had to flee from Strassburg when the *Rat*, fearful of the imperial wrath, asked him to leave the city for the sake of the common good. To Bucer this must have seemed like a repetition of his flight from Weiszenburg twenty-six years earlier. There was a difference, however, this time. He left as an exile but had become, in the minds of many, "the third German reformer."[9]

The Reformation in Strassburg

Strassburg, at the beginning of the sixteenth century, was one of the most important German imperial cities.[10] It traced its history back to 16 A.D., when it was a Roman settlement named Argentoratum. The Strassburg Oaths of 842 were an augury of things to come, for from that day to recent days the allegiance of Strassburg was fated to shift from one side of the Rhine to the other. Situated on the Rhine, it stood at the crossroads of the commerce between east and west, north and south, and always had been an important commercial and political center. By 1262 it had become a free city and by 1482 it had acquired an exemplary democratic constitution. It was

---

[7] *cf*. McNeill, *op. cit.*, p. 174.
[8] Eells, *op. cit.*, pp. 393-400.
[9] So called by Heinrich Bornkamm in an essay in *Das Jahrhundert der Reformation*, Gottingen, 1966, a reprint of "Martin Bucer's *Bedeutung fur die europäische Reformationsgeschichte*, Schriften des Vereins fur Reformationsgeschichte Nr. 169, Jahrgang 58, Heft 2. Gütersloh, 1952.
[10] The recently published *Deutsche Schriften* (henceforth indicated by D. S. I for Volume I and D. S. II for Volume II) contain many updated facts and sources, based on the most exacting scholarship. Gütersloh & Paris. They have been used extensively. H. Eells' biography, *Martin Bucer*, Yale Univ. Press 1931, is still the best and most reliable. Johann Adam's *Evangelische Kirchengeschichte der Stadt Strassburg*, Strassburg, 1922, is a mine of information based on and quoting extensively from the original manuscripts (henceforth indicated by "Adam").

famous for its beautiful cathedral, begun in 1015 and finished in 1275, the steeple being built during the years 1420 to 1429. St. Thomas, St. Peter and St. Aurelia were already in use as houses of worship by 1100. The Franciscans, Dominicans and Augustinians, and from 1286 the Teutonic Order, were well established and influential in the city. By the end of the fourteenth century Strassburg was served, in addition to the cathedral, by ten churches, 20 chapels, 203 clergy and 30 cloisters which housed 140 monks and 266 nuns.[11] Strassburg proudly claimed as its sons some of the greatest minds and mystics of the later medieval period. Johannes Tauler was born in Strassburg; Meister Eckhardt had been a teacher at the Dominican cloister,[12] and Sebastian Brant, the famous author of *Das Narrenschiff*,[13] first published in Basel, and the same year, 1594, published also in Strassburg in an enlarged edition, was also a native of that city. It was the place of activity of three influential humanists: Geiler von Kaysersberg, Jakob Wimpfeling and Jakob Sturm.[14] Priests and monks were attacked by these men for their immorality and ignorance. The abuses of the Church were ruthlessly exposed, and for this reason, Geiler especially, has been called a "pre-reformer."[15] The fact that Strassburg was also one of the most important publishing and printing centers of Germany was to be of great significance for the future of Protestantism.

The leaders of the Reformation in Strassburg at the time when Bucer arrived were Wolfgang Capito (1478-1531), Matthaeus Zell (1477-1548) and Caspar Hedio (1494-1552). Capito, the son of a blacksmith, was born in Hagenau. He was a humanist and leading Hebrew scholar. Before coming to Strassburg he had been rector and dean of the theological faculty at Basel. In 1519 he became chancellor and preacher at the court of the archbishop of Mainz. Matthaeus Zell, a popular preacher at Strassburg cathedral, was

---

[11] Miriam Usher Chrisman, *Strassburg and the Reform,* New Haven, 1967, is a recent addition to the scholarly investigation of the Strassburg Reformation; *cf.* in this connection, ch. 2. (henceforth cited as Chrisman).
[12] Adam, *op. cit.*, p. 9.
[13] *Ibid.*, pp. 13-15.
[14] *Ibid.*, pp. 11-18.
[15] *Ibid.*, p. 9. Geiler died in 1510.

born at Kaysersberg. He came from a middle class background, was a protégé of Geiler and in 1518 was called to the cathedral in Strassburg. As early as March 15, 1521 he began to preach the gospel. Caspar Hedio, protégé and alter ego of Capito, was born in Ettlingen. He was a self-effacing scholar who faithfully and quietly worked in the shadow of the other two reformers. They were joined in 1523 by Martin Bucer (1491–1551), the son of a cooper and citizen of Strassburg, born and raised in Schlettstadt, thirty miles southwest of Strassburg. Though he was the last one to join the group of three, Bucer's meteoric rise to the preeminent position of leadership of the Reformation in Strassburg is testimony of his dynamic and vigorous personality.

The Life of Martin Bucer (1491–l551)[16]

Martin Bucer was born on November 11, 1491, in the Alsatian town of Schlettstadt. He was eight years younger than Luther and Zwingli, older than Melanchthon by six years and older than Calvin by eighteen years. His parents (a Kubler or barrelmaker—some say a shoemaker— and a midwife) lived in considerable poverty with his paternal grandfather but later moved to Strassburg (where his father became a citizen), leaving the ten-year-old Martin in Schlettstadt with his grandfather. Martin attended the Lateinschule, proved himself an apt student and leaned eagerly toward humanism. At the age of fifteen he entered the Dominican monastery in Schlettstadt, hoping to pursue his classical studies, but found over the next ten years that he hated the monastic life and despised the Dominican fount of all knowledge, Thomas Aquinas.[17] Finally, at the age of twenty-five, he was transferred to the Dominican monastery in Heidelberg, which had been founded as an institution for theological study in close connection with the

---

[16] In addition to Eells, for the early life of Bucer I have used the chronology of D. S. I and II; for details of his life, the various introductory notes to his many writings. Especially valuable are the autobiographical references in *Summary seiner Predig in Weissenburg* (henceforth *Summary*), D. S. I, pp. 79-147, especially pp. 125-147; and two defenses, *Verantwortung M. Butzers* to the *Rat* on June 17-19, 1523, D. S. II:293-301, and the longer one for the general public, D. S. I:156-184, published in the fall of 1523.

[17] Eells, *op.cit.*, p. 3.

university. By this time, however, there was bitter enmity between the two institutions, for "the Dominicans championed the dogmas of medieval scholasticism, while many of the university professors were famous leaders of humanism."[18] Bucer's scholarship in Greek and Latin was once more able to advance through the courses which he took at the university. For a time he was able to study under the very popular professor Johannes Brenz and in 1519 he completed the degrees of Bachelor of Theology and Master of Students.

In April, 1518, he was present when Martin Luther came to Heidelberg to defend himself and his ninety-five theses concerning the abuse of indulgences.[19] So greatly was he influenced that in the following months he became Luther's staunch supporter in increasingly active correspondence, teaching and disputations. Unafraid of the enemies he made, Bucer championed both Luther and humanists like Reuchlin, von Hutten and Erasmus, until at last in November, 1520, he found himself forced to flee from the monastery. He was at once aided by Maternus Hatten of Speyer and by Ulrich von Hutten and Franz von Sickingen at the Ebernburg. Fortunate in having obtained his release from the monastic vows before his enemies could exert their influence against him, he was placed in the ranks of the secular clergy and given the right to hold any type of clerical position.[20] His first activity was connected with the Diet of Worms, in which he served as dispatch-bearer between the knightly estate known as the Ebernburg, where Ulrich von Hutten was residing as the guest of Franz von Sickingen, and the city of Worms, to which Luther had been called to appear before his superiors. The messages he bore did not dissuade Luther from appearing at the Diet, as von Hutten had hoped, and the young Bucer's time in Worms was soon employed in writing. He published a *Dialogue between a Pastor and a Village Mayor*, which proved popular enough to run through thirteen editions.[21] About this time (April 1521) Bucer stepped into the position of chap-

---

[18] Eells, *op. cit.*, p. 3.
[19] *Ibid.*, p. 4.
[20] Eells, *op.cit.*, p.9
[21] Eells, *op.cit.*, p. 10.

lain at the court of Count Frederick of the Palatinate, who at that time resided in Worms. The count, together with his several brothers, four of whom later became bishops, had been raised by the humanist, Reuchlin.[22]

However, Count Frederick was not a likely target for Lutheran influence, as Bucer had hoped, for in his position as president of the Imperial Council of Regency "it was his duty to enforce the Edict of Worms, not transgress it by nourishing a Lutheran group under his own roof."[23] Bucer must have found the glittering court life to be unfruitful soil for the sowing of the gospel, for by the end of one year he again sought the aid of von Hutten and von Sickingen to grant him an opportunity to follow the dictates of his calling. Von Sickingen offered him a parish at Landstuhl in April 1522. While in Landstuhl Bucer took the very decisive step of marrying. Moreover, he married a former nun, Elizabeth Silbereisen. When Franz von Sickingen's daring attempt to lead a revolt of German knights against the Elector of Treves ended in ruin for both himself and von Hutten, Bucer and his wife left the parish of Landstuhl. Bucer was most eager to continue his studies at Wittenberg, and planned first to take his wife to his parental home in Strassburg, but along the way he yielded to the pleas of Heinrich Motherer, a pastor in Weissenburg,[24] to stay and preach the gospel to his parishioners. Bucer, aroused so much enthusiasm for the Reformation in Weissenburg, that by the end of six months his enemies succeeded in getting both Bucer and Motherer excommunicated, this despite the fact that Bucer had been released from his monastic vows more than two years earlier,[25] and as a secular cleric, had powerful friends. The Council of Weissenburg, fearful of reprisals against all the town because of the evangelical preaching to which the people had listened so eagerly, secretly requested that Bucer, his wife and Motherer leave. They quietly fled that city one night in May 1523. Franz von Sickingen had been willing to underwrite Bucer's expenses for continu-

---

[22] *Neue Deutsche Biographie, herausgegeben* v.d. Historischen Kommission bei der Bayerischen Akademie der Wissenschaft. Vol. V, p. 529. Duncker & Huōnblot, Berlin, 1960.
[23] Eells, *op.cit.*, p.11.
[24] For the background of the events surrounding Bucer's stay in Weissenburg, *cf*. D.S. I, pp. 71-75.
[25] The letter of dismissal, dated Feb. 20, 1521, is found in D. S. I, pp. 286-290.

ing education at Wittenberg, and since the entire stay in Weissenburg had actually occurred as an interlude along the way, one might expect that Bucer would now proceed to carry out the plans. He did indeed take his wife to visit his parents in Strassburg, but he never did go on to further studies in Wittenberg.

Immediately upon his arrival in Strassburg, the bishop of the city demanded from the *Rat* that, since Bucer was a renegade monk, had married a nun and was a heretic, he should be expelled. Bucer appealed to the *Rat* by citing the Strassburger citizenship of his father and on May 18th he was granted the protection of the city. He stayed for a time at the home of Capito, and almost immediately began to lecture and to preach. So popular were both undertakings that the *Rat*, fearing an uproar, prohibited his lecturing in German and directed him to continue in Latin. The church of St. Aurelia, situated in the western part of the city, just within the city walls, and most of whose members were gardeners, took the unheard-of step of electing Bucer as their minister on March 29, 1524. The *Rat* took the equally unheard-of step of confirming this election on April 4th. Bucer remained their pastor until 1531, when he became pastor of St. Thomas (which today is the cathedral church of French Protestantism) where he served from 1531 to 1540. By the end of the year 1525 Bucer had become the undisputed leader and spokesman of the Strassburg reformers.

As early as the end of 1524 it was Bucer who wrote *Grund und Ursach* in the name of the Strassburg preachers who co-signed the writing. By 1530 he was elected president of the newly founded Church Council, the supreme ecclesiastical authority in Strassburg, and in 1533, under his leadership, the *Sixteen Articles* and the *Confessio Tetrapolitana*, were adopted as the authoritative theological position of Strassburg.[26] The years 1524 to 1531 found Bucer, the Erasmian humanist, busy establishing a sound educational system for the children and young people of Strassburg. So valuable was this revolutionary aspect of his work that the Strassburg physician, Gereon Sailer, in a letter of November 11, 1539, could say to Philip of Hesse: "If he (Bucer)

---

[26] Eells, *op. cit.*, pp. 146-159.

had done nothing else during his life but establish schools in Strassburg, it would have been a glorious and God-pleasing accomplishment."[27]

Eight proposals of the years 1524 to 1531 are now found in *Deutsche Schriften*.[28] Bucer's efforts in the field of education culminated in the publication, in June 1531, of *Christenlich Leeren, Ceremonien und Leben*,[29] which represents a landmark in the organization of schools in Strassburg. The express goal of this writing was to make provision for an educated ministry characterized by enlightened piety. To a large extent the organization and purpose of Protestant education, as expressed and developed in Strassburg by John Sturm, who became rector of the Gymnasium in 1538, served as a model for Protestant education in Geneva, Scotland and finally in our own country. The Church in a very true sense had become the mother of education. In Strassburg itself, a home for poor students was established in 1534, the *Paedagogium* in 1535 and finally the *Gymnasium* in 1538. In 1621 Ferdinand II conferred on it the full privileges of a university. The University of Strassburg, which attracted thousands of students from all over Europe and England, had come into being. In this work the Strassburg preachers, and especially Bucer, were the guiding spirits. Another aspect of the ecclesiastical life of Strassburg in which Bucer was intimately involved during the years 1523-1529, was the abolition of the Mass. The *Rat* found itself in the unenviable position of being set upon from three sides: from the bishop, representing the ecclesiastical Roman establishment; from the Emperor, representing the secular power of the Empire; and from the preachers, representing the populace of Strassburg. The *Rat* moved slowly and carefully in this precarious situation.

December 1, 1523 is a logical date for the beginning of the Reformation in Strassburg for on that day the *Rat* ordered that only the true gospel should be preached from the Strassburg pulpits. By 1525 there had been a gradual reduction in the number of masses. On May 31, 1528, only the four main churches still retained the Mass. These were the Cathedral, Young and

---

[27] D.S. II: 392.
[28] D.S. II: 387-422.
[29] D.S. II: 416-417.

Old St. Peter, and St. Thomas. By vote of the *Rat* on February 20, 1529, and in spite of Jacob Sturm, who wrote from the sessions of the Diet of Speyer counseling caution, the Mass was abolished. Ninety-four members of the *Rat* voted that no action be taken, one voted to retain the mass now and forever, and one hundred and eighty-four voted that "the Mass be abolished until it could be proved that it was a pious form of worship."[30] Strassburg had become a Protestant city. The record of the efforts of the Strassburg preachers in abolishing the mass is preserved in a series of constant reminders to the *Rat* between 1522 and 1529, fifteen of which have been printed for the first time in *Deutsche Schriften*.[31] Two of these deal with justification for reform, seven are writings against the Mass, and six are proposals for the renovation of public worship. Number fifteen, published about 1529, is the most comprehensive, giving a detailed historical survey of the efforts of the preachers.[32]

The contents of these proposals are particularly important because they reflect the basic attitude and even the phraseology of Bucer as it was first stated in *Grund und Ursach*. The arguments of these proposals for the abolition of the Mass are as follows: The Mass is contrary to the Word of God and therefore an invention of the human mind. The Mass is a dreadful blasphemy *(greuliche Gotteslasterung)* because it teaches the common man to place his trust in a "good work," and is profitable to and exploited by the priests. Trust should be placed in God alone and in the redemption won for us by the benefits of the death of Christ, Who died once for all. The Mass was unknown in the ancient church. There is constant call for public debate with the representatives of the Roman Catholic Church. Bucer's hand in these proposals is seen in the willingness of the preachers to pay with their lives "in a three-fold way" if their teachings[33] are proven to be wrong and not in accordance with Holy Scripture.

---

[30] Chrisman, *op. cit.,* page 172.
[31] D.S. II, pp. 423.
[32] D.S. II, pp.546-558.
[33] Bucer's repeated insistence in *Summary, cf.* pp. 137-138.

Every means should be used to abolish the Mass, first by the citizens, who should show their protest by absenting themselves from the Mass and by constant supplication to the *Rat*, and secondly by the authorities, whose duty as Christian authorities obliges them to implement reforms regardless of internal and external political consequences. "We must obey God alone." New forms of worship must be constantly proposed, discussed and finally introduced. If the reforms are not introduced and the mass is not abolished, the wrath of God will visit the city. Chrisman suggests[34] that the most forceful of these arguments were the lack of scriptural warrant for the mass and the threat of the wrath of God. It seems more likely that an informed and aggressive "lobby," using all of the arguments mentioned above, finally achieved the abolition of the mass in Strassburg. It is quite obvious that the guiding hand and spirit behind all these efforts were Bucer's. From 1528 until the end of his life Bucer spent himself in the pursuit of his magnificent obsession to establish union. His union efforts were two-pronged. One prong was his concern for union among divided Protestants; the other was his concern to achieve union between Protestants and Catholics.

From 1525 to 1528 Bucer was an aggressive Zwinglian. His move in the direction of a Lutheran rapprochement came with his reading of Luther's *Vom Abendmahl Christi, Bekenntnis,* published in 1528.[35] Luther's concept of "sacramental union"[36] was adopted by Bucer with a passionate hope that the secret for achieving union between the south Germans and the Lutherans had been found; and although Luther, at the Marburg Colloquy in 1529,[37] counted Bucer among his opponents, he had no idea that Bucer was already moving in his direction. It seems possible that at the same conference Melanchthon was moving in the direction of Bucer. Several times dur-

---

[34] Chrisman, p. 173. Chapter 10 is an excellent account of the abolition of the mass, containing many valuable and new sources.
[35] W.A. XVVII, 261ff.
[36] *Cf.* Eells, *op. cit.*, 287-91.
[37] W. Köhler, *Zwingli und Luther,* vol. I, 1924, Vol. I, 1953, Gütersloh, is the most comprehensive treatment of this subject. Vol. I is summarized in W. Köhler, *Das Religionsgesprach zu Marburg 1529;* Tübingen, 1929; Hermann Sasse, *This is my Body,* Minneapolis, 1959, pp. 187-344.

ing the Colloquy the weary Luther turned to Melanchthon, asking him to continue the discussion, but Melanchthon remained silent. Does this silence indicate that, as a result of the private discussions between Bucer and Melanchthon during this conference, Melanchthon was beginning to have doubts?

During 1529 and 1530, to be sure, in the Augsburg Confession of 1530 and the Apology, Melanchthon is publicly in full agreement with Luther. Soon, however, the acquaintanceship between Bucer and Melanchthon ripened into friendship and collaboration, resulting in suspicion on the part of Luther toward Melanchthon and an unhappy relationship between the two, beginning with 1538.[38] Bucer's great genius in his union efforts lay partly in his temperament, which faced insurmountable difficulties with indomitable courage and deathless optimism and partly in his ability to find and to express union formulae. In the sacramental controversies this was of the greatest importance because the formulae simplified complex problems, were easy to remember and seemed to solve difficulties. However, Calvin's clear insight perceived the dangers involved,[39] the danger of oversimplification, the danger of vagueness, so that opposing parties could interpret the same terms in diametrically opposing fashion, and also that in the end the formulae might breed suspicion and hostility, eventually nullifying the original intent.

The suspicion of Luther toward Bucer and later on the hatred of the Zwinglians toward Bucer illustrate the fate of the "union" man who walks the via media. Bucer's motives, as Calvin clearly saw, were pure and above reproach, all for "the promotion of the Kingdom of Christ," conditioned as they were by spiritual, practical, political, psychological and pastoral considerations. Calvin also noted that as a consequence "Bucer loads himself with the hatred of many."[40] The divided state of Protestantism found ex-

---

[38] *Cf.* H. Jacoby, *Die Liturgik der Reformatoren,* especially Vol. 11: *Liturgik Melanchthons,* par. 38-42.

[39] *Cf.* Calvin's letters of May ll and 12, 1541, written to Farel from the sessions of the Diet at Regensburg. J. Bonnet, *Letters of Calvin,* Vol. I, pp. 236-240.

[40] *Cf.* Calvin's letters to Farel from the sessions of the Diet at Regensburg. J. Bonnet, *Letters of Calvin* Vol. I, pp. 236-240.

pression in the presentation of three different confessions to the emperor at the Diet of Augsburg in 1530: the *Augsburg Confession* by the Lutherans,[41] the *Tetrapolitana* by Bucer, and the *Fidei Ratio* by Zwingli. The *Wittenberg Concord* of 1536 united the Lutherans and the south Germans but separated both from the Swiss, who suspected duplicity particularly in the statement that Christ is "substantially present."[42] Union of the Swiss was finally accomplished by Calvin and Bullinger in the *Consensus Tigurinas,* 1549; but the Swiss and the Lutherans henceforth continued to go their separate ways.

The attempted introduction of the Reformation into Cologne[43] was another of Bucer's failures. The bishop of Cologne, Herman von Wied, called Bucer to Bonn in December, 1542. The proposals of the Cologne Reformation, in which Melanchthon was a collaborator, were published in 1543 as the *Einfältiges Verdenken.* However, as a result of the fierce opposition of the majority of the Cologne ecclesiastical establishment and of the Emperor himself, the Reformation in Cologne failed.[44] Cologne remained Catholic, von Wied shortly afterward was excommunicated and retired to his ancestral estate where he died. Bucer's efforts to unite Protestants and Catholics too were destined to fail. He was commissioned by the Emperor to take a leading part in the discussions at Regensburg, Hagenau and Worms from June, 1540 to April, 1541. Again, in 1546 at Regensburg Bucer was involved in further discussions with the Spanish theologians, and again in 1548 his services were demanded at Augsburg. The Emperor, esteeming the abilities of Bucer in union discussions but overestimating Bucer's willingness to compromise his basic convictions at any price even at the price of union with the Catholics, was furious when Bucer secretly departed from the discussions and published his position in "Ein Summarischer Vergritf."[45] The Emperor demanded that the Strassburg *Rat* punish Bucer. When Bucer con-

---

[41] Representing the position of the four cities of Strassburg, Constance, Memmingen and Lindau.
[42] McNeill, *op. cit.*, pp.159-161.
[43] *Cf.* Eells, *op. cit.*, pp. 321-337, esp. pp. 334-335. also Adam, *op. cit.*, pp. 250-251.
[44] *Cf.* Mechtild Kohn, *Martin Bucers Entwurf einer Reformation des Erzstifts Köln,* Luther Verlag, Witten, 1966.
[45] Eells, *op. cit.*, p.396ff.

tinued to express himself loudly and clearly the *Rat*, fearful of incurring the displeasure and punishment of the Emperor, asked Bucer to leave Strassburg.

From among the many offers of refuge which came to Bucer from Wittenberg, Geneva, Copenhagen and other places, Bucer chose to accept the invitation of Archbishop Cranmer to go to England. He arrived in London with his younger colleague, Paul Fagius, in April, 1549. Edward VI wished them to translate the Bible from the original into Latin. Later both men went to Cambridge as professors. Fagius died very soon, but Bucer lectured very successfully, wrote his last work, *De Regno Christi*, received an honorary doctorate from Cambridge University, and died after a short illness in 1551. He was buried with great honors at Cambridge, but during the reign of Queen Mary his body was exhumed and publicly burned. Queen Elizabeth, however, again honored his memory in 1560.[46]

The Occasion for Writing *Grund und Ursach* The year 1524 was a decisive year in the progress of the Reformation in Strassburg.[47] It was marked by uncertainty, tension, confusion and fear in many quarters. Fear was caused by the threat of Strassburg's involvement in the Peasants War, which had enflamed Swabia and brought distress to country life surrounding Strassburg. Refugees and exiles were beginning to arrive in Strassburg, which had a reputation for hospitality and toleration. Tensions were caused by the conflicts with the various opposing groups in the city itself. Bucer's confrontation with Conrad Treger[48] and Thomas Murner[49] were symptomatic of the confrontation between the old established religion and the reformation. The estrangement between the humanists and the reformers as a result of Erasmus' cautious and negative attitude to the Reformation[50] was evident in similar attitudes of Wimpfeling, Rhenatus and other humanists.

---

[46] *Ibid.*, pp. 413-414.
[47] *Cf.* Chrisman, *op. cit.*, chapters 6-12, pp. 81 if; for the years 1524-25 cf. pp. 155-176; *cf.* also Eells, *op. cit.*, chapter v, pp. 33ff.
[48] *Cf.* "Hnadel mit Conrad Treger", D. S. 11, pp. 37-173; also D. S. 11, p. 33, n73.
[49] *Cf.* Adam, *op. cit.*, chapter 6, pp. 75ff.
[50] The publication of *De Libero Arbitrio* in 1524; *cf.* also Eells, *op. cit.*, pp. 40-42.

The arrival of both Carlstadt[51] and Hinne Rode[52] in the city in the fall added to the confusion. Hinne Rode's letter from Honius and Carlstadt's peculiar teaching on the sacraments aroused confusion among the people and consternation among the Reformers. Both men forced the Reformers to re-examine their understanding of the sacraments. Urgent letters were sent to Wittenberg and Zurich, seeking light and guidance in this confusion. Gerbel, an important member of the *Rat* and a life-long friend of Luther's in a letter of November 22[53] informed Luther of the troublesome situation in Strassburg. The following day the Reformers, too, sent a letter to Luther[54] in which they asked for Luther's advice. Capito, fearing the possibility of disastrous consequences for the progress of the reformation in Strassburg, sent a letter to the Christians[55] counseling them to stand fast despite the conflict between Luther and Carlstadt in which they had become involved. It is significant that this letter and the letter of the preachers to Luther show remarkable similarities with *Grund und Ursach* indicating the common authorship of Bucer (at least his guiding hand) and the united front of the Strassburg preachers.

In some areas questions were being raised regarding the radical liturgical reform which was taking place in Strassburg. Soon after Theobald Schwarz conducted the first German Mass on February 16, 1524, Bucer had been busy reforming the Strassburg liturgies.[56] In his own church images were removed, and the shrine of St. Aurelia, a former center of reverence and pilgrimage, was destroyed.[57] Many innovations and changes in the liturgy were introduced, and many old established customs and practices in connection with the observance of the sacraments, were abolished. In order to defend these radical changes and to justify these reforms by offering

---

[51] on Carlstadt, *cf.* below, pp. 233-237.
[52] on Hinne Rode, *cf.* below, pp. 238-240.
[53] W. A. Br. III, 378-380.
[54] W. A. Br. III, 381-387.
[55] Walch XX: 340-351.
[56] On Bucer's liturgical reform, cf. below, The Shape of the Strassburg Liturgy, pp. 266 ff.
[57] *Grund und Ursach*, translation, par. 174-176, pp. 204-206.

scriptural proof and by expounding the theological rationale of the doctrine of the sacraments, Bucer wrote *Grund und Ursach*.

Background and Overview of *Grund Und Ursach*

Grund und Ursach is considered by some scholars to be Bucer's most important and significant work.[1] To all intents and purposes it was a statement of faith of the Strassburg reformers. Its main purpose is to defend and justify the innovations which had been introduced in Strassburg as being firmly grounded in the Holy Scriptures. Its great importance among all Reformation writings lies in giving us insight into the methods and spirit in which reform came to one of the great medieval cities, Strassburg, which can probably serve as a prototype of the introduction of the Reformation in other cities — this quite apart from its primary importance, namely as a confession of faith of the Strassburg reformers.

The Covering Letter

The covering letter accompanying *Grund und Ursach* is addressed to His Serene Highness and Illustrious Prince and Lord, Friedrich, Count Palatine of the Rhine. He was a member of the Imperial Governing Council *(Reichsregimenti)*, was an accomplished courtier, nobly born and intimately involved with the political activities of the Hapsburg House. Bucer had been in the employ of Count Frederick from April, 1521 to April, 1522, had been with his court at Worms and in Nürnberg and, asking for his release, had been dismissed by the Count with good wishes, accompanied by presents and promises of help in the future. Count Frederick, although he did not actually lean toward the evangelical movement, had nevertheless shown no inclination to make a stand against it. Ostensibly one of the reasons for the *Sendschreiben* is to explain the evangelical innovations in Strassburg and to give the justification and reason *(Grund und Ursach)* for these in the Word of God, and further to state in summary fashion the teachings of the Strass-

---

[1] *e.g.* Baum: *Grund und Ursach* is among the most solid and most courageous writings to come from his pen. W. Baum *Capito und Butzer*, p. 289.

burg reformers. It becomes obvious, however, that there are additional reasons.

One of these is to attack the so-called spiritual leaders, the princes and the priests, for the luxury, voluptuousness and immorality of their lives. They should be shining examples of the true Christian life but instead, using the privileges of their offices, they encourage and exploit the superstitions of the common people to their own personal profit. In a sweeping condemnation Bucer says that there is "nothing healthy and whole in the entire spiritual estate." Another purpose is to answer the accusations of the opponents of the Reformation, who say that such revolutionary behavior is opposed to regularly constituted authority. Bucer points out to Frederick that it has been the spiritual leaders, since the last *Reichstag*,[2] who have used all the powers at their disposal to suppress all those who advocate reforms. He mentions repeatedly their practice of condemnation without a hearing and a trial. Bucer very pointedly affirms that final authority belongs to God However the rightful function and place of the civil authorities in the *societas christiana* is to implement Christian reform, to suppress lawlessness and heresy, and to work in closest harmony with the evangelical reformers.[3] A third reason for the *Sendschreiben* is to reply to personal calumnies directed against the reformers, but especially against Bucer.

We are most fortunate to have available now the published manuscripts which give autobiographical details about Bucer's life.[4] The most valuable of these are two "Justifications," one of which Bucer personally presented to the *Rat* from June 17–20, 1523,[5] which he decided to publish in extended form in the fall of that same year.[6] From these we learn that three basic ac-

---

[2] Edict of Nürnberg, March 23, 1523 (referred to in Bucer's *Summary*, D. S. I:136.
[3] Bucer is not only addressing Count Frederick, but also by indirection the Strassburg *Rat*.
[4] *Summary*, D. S. I:79-146.
[5] *Verantwortung vor dem Rat*, D. S. I:293-301.
[6] D. S. I, pp. 156-184. This rather detailed reference concludes with an extensive autobiographical passage describing his life from age fifteen until the fall of 1523. He lists as witnesses to a life above reproach the Dominican monks, among whom he had spent 15 of his 32 years, Count Frederick of the Palatine and his court, Franciscus von Sickingen, the *Rat* and the congregation at Weissenburg, and finally the *Rat* and the citizens of Strassburg. (p. 181)

cusations were directed against Bucer: One was that he was a renegade monk, to which Bucer replies that he was released from his vows by the Bishop of Speyer on April 29, 1521.[7] The second accusation, that he had married a nun, Bucer answers by saying that the married life is biblical and natural, while the life of the monks and nuns is unbiblical and unnatural. A third accusation, that he preaches heresy, Bucer answers by saying that *scriptura sola* has been the only source of his preaching and teaching and that his only concern is to serve the neighbor.

In August, 1523, Bucer had also summarized the contents of his preaching at Weissenburg, presenting this to the Strassburg *Rat* as proof of his scriptural orthodoxy. The purpose of the *Sendschreiben* in this regard, then, was to cite as a favorable witness, by implication, Count Frederick of the Palatine, who had known Bucer intimately as his chaplain and a member of his court for twelve months. Again by implication (Bucer had been honorably dismissed with the goodwill and gifts of the Count), the *Sendschreiben* intended to point out that Bucer still retained the Count's favorable interest when, two and one-half years later, he wrote *Grund und Ursach*.

Finally, he expresses the hope that the Count will stand firm in his evangelical convictions, adding the not too subtle hint that his Highness should support the interests and efforts of the Strassburg reformers. In many respects, then, the *Sendschreiben* is used by Bucer as a "letter of recommendation" with the intent of reaching a wide, sympathetic audience at a time when this practice would have far reaching effects for the cause of the Reformation in the Palatinate.

Basic Principles of *Grund Und Ursach*

Certain themes appear and reappear constantly in *Grund und Ursach*. They are: the importance of the Word of God, of faith, of love, of the Holy Spirit and of Christian freedom. All five are closely interrelated and logically interdependent, and are used by Bucer to interpret his doctrine of the sacraments, the use and reform of practices and usages in connection with wor-

---

[7] Given in Latin, D. S. I:285-290.

ship, with the basic meaning of the liturgy and in the various other reforms or innovations which were made in Strassburg during 1524. The first and most important principle is the supreme importance of the Word of God. By it all innovations are justified and all abuses condemned. Anything contrary to the Word of God must go. It contains all that is good and useful, and anything added to it is from the devil. It is impartial and has no regard for persons. In it the Strassburg preachers find the only source and norm of their teaching, their preaching, their reforms. It contains the whole counsel of God and must be obeyed implicitly. Bucer quotes extensively from the Old and the New Testaments, and the realization comes with a pleasant shock, that most of those who originally read *Grund und Ursach* probably heard the words of the Bible in German for the first time.[8]

The commands of Moses are important, and yet are subordinated to Christ, Who throws light on Moses—Christ Who has set us free. His "biblicism" is strangely and surprisingly inconsistent. In dealing with the abolition of the elevation and holy days, for example, the Old Testament seems to be of primary importance, when it would have been much more obvious to use New Testament justifications. Quite often, after stating his interpretation of some biblical passage, he will say, "Be that as it may...for me it is enough." At times his exegesis seems forced, and then at other times it is remarkably modern.[9] But constantly and consistently, when concern for the weaker brethren, and the need to make...[10]

---

[8] A list of Bucer's books, compiled on April 30, 1518, lists: *Novum Testamentum graece et latine per Erasmum castigtum et ejusdem adnotiones in illud, uno volumine* (He may also have had available Luther's translation of the N. T.); *Paraphrasis in Epistolam ad Romanos Erasmi; Psalterium hebraicum, cum adscripto latino ex tralatione S. Hieronymi, minuto libello ac plane manuali*. The major works of Erasmus and several Latin, Greek and Hebrew grammars and lexicons are also found in the list. (*Deutsche Schriften* I, 281-284).

[9] Modern New Testament scholarship would agree that in John 6:35–50 there are sacramental undertones. In regard to the eucharistic interpretation of John 6:63, scholarship is divided. *Cf.* Raymond E. Brown, *The Gospel of John,* Doubleday, 1966, pp. 281-303, for recent treatment and summary of various interpretations.

[10] Editor's note: the sentence is not complete in Cypris's commentary.

The second basic principle is Bucer's concept of faith. Here again his dependence on Luther is apparent.[11] This dependence is revealed particularly in the first two of Bucer's early writings,[12] but not entirely lacking in *Grund und Ursach*. Bucer was not a blind follower of Luther.[13] To be sure, basic to *Grund und Ursach* are *sola scriptura, sola gratia* and *sola fide,* but *fides* is somewhat modified. True faith is a gift of God and comes to us through the Word of God. The content of our faith is that Christ died once for all for the forgiveness of sins.[14] Through His death the elect are cleansed, saved and justified.[15] This death of Christ has an eternal validity.

Bucer's constant use of this theme of the *theologia crucis* in *Grund und Ursach*, echoing the teaching of the "young Luther," basic to all the reformers, sounds like a scholastic formulation, where *fiducia* seems to be overshadowed by *assensus* and becomes *persuasio*.[16] This seems to be confirmed by his saying, "He who does not believe this is not a true Christian."[17] The purpose of the sacraments is to strengthen faith and to rekindle true love. In the *Summary* he says "True faith is the work of God and the fulfilling of all His laws."[18] At the same time the realization of God's overwhelming love and mercy in accepting the elect, "the lambs of Christ," over whom He watches with loving care, leads to praise and thanksgiving in life and in worship and expresses itself in active love.

The third basic principle is love. It is closely identified with faith and usually pared with faith.[19] It is one of the outstanding and "formal" princi-

---

[11] In D. S. I, 39, J. Muller points out that whereas Luther's approach to justification is the theological dialectic of faith: *simul Justus ac peccator,* Bucer's approach is expressed in psychological pedagogical categories in an *ordo justificationis,* as e. g. in the Ephesian Commentary, where the four stages are listed as *Erwablung, Berufung, Heiligung, Verherrlichung*.

[12] *Das Ym Selbs and Summary*.

[13] *Cf.* D. S. I, 38, n. 18.

[14] The once-for-all death of Christ is a constantly recurring theme in *Grund und Ursach*.

[15] The assurance certainty of election is provided by a) the revelation that the elect know that they belong to the lambs of Christ know His voice, the result of love of the Word of God, and b) the willingness to deny the self. D. S. I, 40.

[16] *Cf.* Pauck, *op. cit.*, p. 381, n. 9.

[17] *Grund und Ursach*, p. 144.

[18] D. S. I, 90.

[19] Baum singles out as an outstanding characteristic of Bucer's theology the pairing of *fides et caritas*. On Luther's pairing of faith and love, cf. Vilmos Vatja, *Die Theologie des*

ples of Bucer's theology.[20] Torrance suggests that this "charismatic element" in Bucer's theology may be due "in part to his religious inheritance in Strassburg."[21] Warm piety and mystic inclinations had always been at home there. To Bucer the priesthood of believers means primarily the Christian being Christ to his neighbor. Faith and love are the best spiritual adornments of the Christian. Hindrances to faith and love are from the devil and must be rooted out. Quarrels and disputes, particularly those about words, break the bond of love. A Christian must show his love in a special way by concern for the weaker brethren. He is perfectly justified in making concessions in the interpretation and application of *adiaphora* for the sake of the weaker brethren. The souls of men must be won with love and patience and by the example of loving concern.

Unlike Carlstadt,[22] and in full agreement with Luther, Bucer believes that innovations and reforms must be introduced slowly and gently for the sake of the weaker brethren, who must not be frightened away by unreasonable demands or radical and sudden changes. Bucer makes concessions even in the application of the ban, "for a while," until through extensive and thorough preaching and teaching the masses are led to a fuller insight into the truth. Again and again he defends himself against the criticism of his opponents, who feel that there must be no concessions at all in this re-

---

Gottesdienstes bei Luther, Gottingen, 1952, pp. 316-352.

[20] D. S. I, 76 (*das Doppelgebot*).

[21] T. F. Torrance, *Kingdom and Church,* London, 1956, p. 74. characterizes Bucer as the "eschatology of love" (Luther's is the eschatology of faith and Calvin's the eschatology of hope). The extent of the influence of *Ein deutsch Theologie* on Bucer, and the many parallels to it, in *Summary* are listed in D. S. I, 94.

[22] *Cf.* Luther's intense reaction to Carlstadt's Wittenberg "reforms" during Luther's enforced stay at the Wartburg, and Carlstadt's reply in *Ob man gemach faren und des ergernüssen der schwachen verschonen soll / in sachen so gottis willen angehn,* printed in Basel, November 1524, reprinted in Erich Hertsch's *Karlstadts Schritten aus den Jahren 1523-25,* Teil I, Halle (Salle) 1956. This book contains eight of Carlstadt's writings, and it is a point of interest to note that one of these is a sermon, printed in Strassburg, October 1524, entitled *Von den zweyen höchsten gebottender lieb gottes und des nechsten...* It is based on Matt. 22:34-40. An adequate life of Carlstadt, free from all denominational prejudices, has still to be written. C. F. Jäger's is entirely inadequate and Hermann Barge's (Leipzig, 1905) is still the best. A recent excellent attempt is found in Gordon Rupp's *Patterns of Reformation,* Philadelphia, 1969, pp. 49-153.

gard. Although at times Bucer expresses his distrust of the "common man," yet he feels that in the end the masses will respond to the teaching and the example of the elect and, in the end, make the changes of their own accord. "For the sake of the weaker brethren" echoes and re-echoes throughout *Grund und Ursach*. This emphasis on love is a typical theme of all of Bucer's early writings. In an eloquent passage at the conclusion of *"Das Ym Selbs"* we find: "For the Word of God alone is able to make us healthy and whole, and to save us. It produces faith, faith love, and love good works; the final outcome is an eternal heritage and a godly and pious life."[23]

Here, then was the answer of the reformers to the current criticism that the doctrine of *sola fide* would lead to moral and ethical anarchy and libertinism. For an outsider the actions of sectarians, the Spiritualists and even many of the ordinary Protestants would seem to corroborate this accusation. The corrective, however, is found in the teaching of Bucer (and of Luther, and of Carlstadt) that love must become active in good works which are the result of the grateful recognition of God's boundless love and mercy in the Creation, the Incarnation, and in the Atonement. "Faith is strengthened and becomes active through love and good works."[24] Through the sacraments faith is strengthened and love rekindled.[25] So important was this paring of faith and love to Bucer, that at the very end of *Grund und Ursach*, as if to emphasize its supreme importance, he states that the Strassburg preachers direct all their preaching "to the end that faith in God and love to the neighbor, which are the sources of true morality and constant patience, should always be planted, increased and strengthened in our listeners, and that everyone should use external ceremonies…. [F]or the growth of faith and love."[26] In *Grund und Ursach* faith and love have the final word.

The fourth principle is the importance of the Holy Spirit.[27] The Word, faith, love and the Holy Spirit form an indivisible unity. Bucer, quoting John

---

[23] D.S. I, 67.
[24] *Grund und Ursach*, p. 153.
[25] *Ibid.*, pp. 142, 144, *etc.*
[26] *Ibld.*, p. 214.
[27] *Cf.* W. P. Stephens, *The Holy Spirit in the Theology of Martin Bucer,* Cambridge, 1970, which treats this whole subject in detail and with thoroughness.

6:63, insists over and over again that the content of the preaching in Strassburg is that "it is the Spirit which gives life."[28] Those who believe in Christ, he maintains, receive the Holy Spirit,[29] and Christ through His Spirit cleanses, gives faith and saves the elect.[30] It is also the Holy Spirit, he says, who "destroys all sins with fire and purifies and refines the inner man like gold."[31] He even implies that whoever does not have the Spirit is not a Christian,[32] for it is through the Spirit that faith grows stronger and becomes active through love and good works, and through the same Spirit we are bound in love to God and to one another.[33] Without the Spirit the sacraments are empty signs: bread is bread, wine is wine, and water is water.[34] The servants of the Spirit are enabled through the Spirit to render to God that spiritual worship which is acceptable to Him, a worship which concerns itself not with external matters but with inner spiritual realities.[35]

Bucer's emphasis on the inner spiritual aspects of Worship is closely connected with the fifth basic principle, the freedom of the Christian man, which has been won through the once-for-all death of Christ.[36] External ceremonies are *adiaphora,* and Bucer often treats them with remarkable freedom. The elevation, the making of the sign of the cross, and other customs and practices of medieval piety are harmful if they encourage hypocrisy, but are not harmful if their true religious intent is understood.[37] Christian freedom in regard to external matters involves concern for the spiritual well-being of each individual. To force anyone to observe or not to observe any practices, either old or new, without an attendant inner conviction, transgresses against the principle of Christian freedom.

---

[28] *Cf.* the following paragraphs in *Grund und Ursach*: 53-57, pp. 112-116; 104, pp. 155-156; 111, p. 160; 116, p. 164; 142, pp. 180-181.
[29] *Ibid.,* par. 121, p. 167; par. 123, p. 169.
[30] *Ibid.,* par. 130, p. 170.
[31] *Ibid.,* par. 124, p. 169.
[32] *Ibid.,* par. 4, p. 56.
[33] *Ibid.,* par. 47, pp. 105-106.
[34] *Ibid.,* par. 127, p. 172.
[35] *Cf. Grund und Ursach,* paragraphs 57, p. 116; 68, p. 126; 75, p. 131; 116, p. 164.
[36] *Ibid.,* paragraphs 37, p. 97; 111-112, pp. 160-161.
[37] *Ibid.,* paragraphs 79-82, pp. 135-139; 93, p. 148; 109, pp. 159-160; 140, p. 179; 187-188, pp. 212-214.

The decisive importance of the Holy Scriptures, of faith, of love, of the Holy Spirit, and of Christian conviction—these are the basic principles of *Grund und Ursach*. They are logically connected and interdependent, and express Bucer's basic theological convictions at the end of the year 1524. In the days to come there were to be some modifications, the most pronounced of these being in his doctrine of the Lord's Supper. However, true to his genius for making formulae, even there he remained true to his basic convictions which had been deepened as a result of his intense involvement in the sacramental controversies. But to the end of his life the supremacy of the Word was his beacon, faith and love the compass, and the influence of the Holy Spirit the dynamic power. And he remained free in the inner depth of his soul, even though at times, for the sake of the weaker brethren, whether Lutheran or Roman Catholic, he was ready to make concessions. Even in his concessions, his magnificent obsession to unite all Christians everywhere in one great, united *societas christiana*, where Christ was king, suffused his whole being. He was first of all *ein Unionsmann*.

The Translation

Text

The text underlying the present translation is contained in *Doktor Martin Luthers Reformationsschriften* by Dr. J. Georg Walch, Volume XX, columns 352-439.[38] It was carefully compared with *Grund und Ursach* in *Martin Bucers Deutsche Schriften* (D. S.), Volume I, Series I, pages 194-278, edited by Robert Stupperich and published in 1960. This is one of the first volumes of the projected *Martini Buceri Opera Omnia*, to consist of Bucer's German and Latin works and letters, published by an international committee made up of Francois Wendel, Ernst Staehelin, Robert Stupperich, Jean Rott and Rodolphe Peter, published in Germany by the Gütersloher Verlagshaus Gerd Mohn and in France by Presses Universitaires de France, Paris.[39] The publi-

---

[38] *Doktor Martin Luthers Sammtliche Schriften, (Neue revidierte Stereotypausgabe)*, St. Louis, Mo. 1904.
[39] To date (1970) five volumes have been published: volumes 1, 2, 3 and 7 of *Deutsche*

cation of Bucer's works, although only a few volumes in this series have appeared so far, fulfills a long-awaited desire of Bucer and Reformation scholars throughout the world. Certainly one of the reasons why Bucer has been so long neglected has been the unavailability of his works, most of which were buried in Strassburg. Another major drawback to the publication of his works has been the illegibility of his script.[40] There have been and presently are very few scholars with the necessary competence to decipher many of his manuscripts. There is no doubt that at last Bucer will come into his own and will occupy a rightful place of importance, which he deserves as one of the great leaders of the Reformation.[41] Except for minor differences in spelling, punctuation, paragraphing, the addition and/or omission of a few words, the texts in the Walch edition and in the *Deutsche Schriften* correspond. There is no original manuscript of *Grund und Ursach* in existence. One of the earliest copies, undated but according to its preface published on December 26, 1524,[42] is in the *Thomasstift* (Collegium Wilhelmitanum) in Strassburg. Another copy, republished in the early days of January 1525, is in the Bibliotheque Nationale et Universitaire of Strassburg. Still another copy is part of the McAlpin Collection at Union Theological Seminary, New York.

Style

The style of *Grund und Ursach* is tortuous and involved. Amongst his contemporaries Bucer was known for his inability to write briefly. It was a common failing in the writings of all the reformers with the exception of Calvin.[43] Bucer's dynamic vigor and impatience are evident in his style. He

---

Schriften, 1960-1970 and volume 15 which contains *De Regno Christi, Martini Buceri Opera Latina*, 1955.

[40] This is illustrated graphically in a collection of microfilmed manuscripts which I placed into the Library of Union Theological Seminary, New York, catalogued as Miscellaneous Liturgical Writings, 1525-1546.

[41] So Pauck, *op. cit.*, p. 74; Torrance, *op. cit.*, p. 73; and J. Pelikan, *Obedient Rebels*, New York, 1964, p. 142, n3.

[42] Information supplied to me by the librarian of the Bibliotheque Nationale et Universitaire.

[43] A perfect example of conciseness is Calvin's *Petit Traicte de la Saincte Cene de nostre Sei-*

quite obviously wrote *Grund und Ursach* in a hurry. Now and then sentences and thoughts are left dangling, probably because his thoughts slipped ahead of his pen.[44] Since *Grund und Ursach* is addressed to the general public (as was the *Sendschreiben*), the tone of the writing is colloquial yet never familiar and, contrary to all the polemical writings of that period, is remarkably free from invective, even though the polemic against the abuses of the Roman Catholic Church and the spiritual leaders is strong. The writing reflects a warm personality with a deep pastoral concern for the spiritual welfare of the members of the community and a disarming depth and warmth of piety.

Punctuation

The punctuation of the manuscript is quite arbitrary. It has been modernized to some extent in the *Deutsche Schriften,* so that the sense is brought out more clearly. Bucer uses the colon regularly to indicate the consequence of the thought previously stated. The German language of this period was in a state of flux and in the process of development, similar to that of pre-Shakespearean English. What Shakespeare's works and the King James Version did for the English language, Luther's translation of the Bible did for the German language almost one hundred years earlier. Since words had not yet settled into a consistent spelling, some words in *Grund und Ursach* are difficult to reconstruct except phonetically, or by research in specialized publications.[45] The customary literary and international language of scholarly discourse was Latin. Bucer, Luther and Zwingli were pioneers in the use of the vernacular in their writings. Their Latin obviously is superior to their German. The influence of Latin is seen in Bucer's involved sentence structure, consisting of main clauses, sub-clauses and sub-sub-clauses, which make the task of the translator most difficult.[46]

---

gneur et seul Sauveur Jesus Christ 1541.

[44] In this translation of *Grund und Ursach,* infelicities of syntax, incomplete sentences, and the like, are reproduced without correction.

[45] Such as the voluminous and exhaustive *Grimms Worterbuch.* Walch's edition (vol. XX) supplies a list of words which are rare or unfamiliar.

[46] *Cf.* W. Pauck's judgment, *Melanchthon and Luther,* Library of Christian Classics, Philadel-

In the translation which follows, I have modernized the punctuation only to the extent of bringing out the exact sense of the original and have stayed as closely as possible to the original in order to reproduce the delightful flavor of the original writing. *Grund und Ursach,* which obviously was written with a hurried urgency, does not seem to have been edited. In spite of this the contents are arranged in an orderly manner and are presented clearly and for the most part concisely.

Bucer's Doctrine of the Sacraments[47]

Historical Background

The sacramental controversies which divided European Protestants into opposing camps were triggered by the arrival of Carlstadt in Strassburg near the end of September, 1524. By temperament and conviction Bucer found himself caught in the middle of this conflict, and suffered all the bitter consequences of this position. The fascinating story of this whole upheaval must be viewed in the context of the Reformation as a whole.

Fateful Correspondence: During the last two decades of the fifteenth century a group of seventeen young humanists, many of whom were later to shed lustre on their city, Strassburg,[48] counted among their number Nicolaus Gerbel,[49] a lawyer who served as an advocate and secretary of the cathedral chapter. As early as 1520 he became a supporter of Luther and kept up a lively correspondence with him, keeping him informed about affairs in Strassburg. He must have written to Luther during the late summer of 1524, for on September 18th of that year Luther wrote him a letter in which he

---

phia, 1969, xx, that Bucer, "who worked hastily and produced much in an astonishingly short time, wrote in an extraordinarily prolix, wordy, and repetitious style, thus causing considerable difficulty for his modern translators." I have attempted, however, to do more than Rupp suggests, viz. "to translate more after the meaning than the words;" *Patterns of Reformation,* Philadelphia, 1969, xiv.

[47] Editor's note: In Cypris's original dissertation this section occurs after the translation.
[48] Chrisman, *op. cit.*, p. 46. Among them: Sebastian Brent, author of *Das Narrenschiff,* Jacob Wimpfeling, Jacob Sturm, Thomas Murner, Hieronymus Gebweiler and Beatus Rhenanus.
[49] *Ibid.*, pp. 81-82.

says, "It is amazing how much I desire to write to the Strassburgers, especially to the preachers; but to write briefly and off the cuff I will not; and to write in detail and at length I cannot, because of the tyranny of my involvements."[50] The close friendship of these men[51] kept the lines of communication open between Strassburg and Wittenberg.[52] In a letter dated December 14, 1524,[53] Luther informs Spalatin that he has received two communications from Strassburg containing disturbing news about the activities of Carlstadt in Strassburg. He tells Spalatin that he will reply to these communications briefly within a few days. True to his word, on December 15th Luther sent his famous "letter of warning" to the Strassburg preachers.[54]

The two communications referred to by Luther were two letters written one day apart and delivered to Luther by the same messenger. So important did the senders consider these letters that this messenger was none other than the deacon of Matthaeus Zell, popular preacher at the cathedral. The earlier of these two letters was written by Nicolaus Gerbel and was dated November 22.[55] He informs Luther of the uproar caused among the common people by the activities of Carlstadt, who had come to Strassburg sometime in October, after having been expelled from his parish in Orlamünde and from Saxony, by the Duke himself, upon the strong advice and suggestion of Luther. Carlstadt had had to leave in such a hurry that his pregnant wife had to remain behind. Gerbel mentions particularly that the confusion was caused by Carlstadt's interpretation of *touto,* namely that when Christ used this word in the institution He had pointed to His body, saying that *touto* referred to His body which was present at that moment in the Upper Room. Gerbel goes on to inform Luther that he, Gerbel, had tried

---

[50] W. A., Br. III, 352.
[51] Later on, Bucer counted him as an opponent, *i. e.,* Gerbel remained faithful to Luther during all the controversies, and stayed on in Strassburg as a teacher of history and law.
[52] Someone should pay tribute to the unsung heroes of the Reformation, the letter carriers! The journey from Wittenberg to Geneva, for example, took twenty days.
[53] W. A., Br. III, 399ff.
[54] W. A., Br. III, 401-403.
[55] W. A., Br. III, 378-380.

his best to calm the people by saying to them that this was only an inconsequential quarrel over words which was harming the faith of many.

The other communication was written on the following day by the Strassburg preachers[56] and told Luther the same story in different words. Carlstadt had made such an impression on the common people that attendance at the regular services was declining.[57] With his sacramental and spiritualistic teaching he had confounded and confused the people. Not only the people were confused, but the preachers themselves had become indecisive about some points of interpretation concerning the Lord's Supper. Carlstadt had emphasized the Johannine saying that "the flesh is of no avail" and applied it to the symbols of the Lord's Supper and Baptism. He had stirred up much indecision; even some in Zurich and Basel seemed to agree with him. The Strassburg preachers could satisfy some of the people with a general answer, but many others were not so easily satisfied and wanted something more definite. Seven of Carlstadt's pamphlets which had been printed in Basel were being read with deepest interest by many people in Strassburg, and the preachers sent along copies of these to Luther. The letter goes on to give a summary of the content of the preaching and some innovations implemented in the service of worship in Strassburg. The words of this summary agree so much with those in *Grund und Ursach* that undoubtedly Bucer is the author of the letter.

Further confusion had been caused in the city by the appearance of Erasmus' latest book,[58] and they condemn Erasmus for causing the advancement of the Kingdom more harm than he ever did it good in earlier days. In fullest trust and confidence they turn to Luther, asking for his ad-

---

[56] W. A., Br. III, 381-387.
[57] Carlstadt was a prolific author. He published 156 writings representing 67 works, of which 18 were published in Latin, 49 in German. Of these Hertzsch (*op. cit.*) reprints eight which were written and published between 1523 and 1525; Walch reprints 5. The most significant book in the sacramental controversies was *Dialogus,* Carlstadt's *Gesprechbüchlein vom Missbrauch der Messe,* published in Basel near the end of October or early November 1524. The "seven writings" mentioned dealt with two topics: (1) Carlstadt's interpretation of the Lord's Supper, (2) reports on his expulsion from Saxony.
[58] Erasmus's *Diatribe de Libero Arbitrio.* Luther's reply, *De servo Arbitrio,* brought about the complete and permanent break between them.

vice and guidance, saying, "Be sure to answer Carlstadt's teaching very carefully, but answer without gall and without anger. . . . Give the impression that you two always have been and now are concerned for the glory of Christ." Luther's reply of December 15th[59] is a condemnation of the activities of Carlstadt in Wittenberg and in Orlamünde. He must be blinded by God, says Luther, to teach as he does about the sacraments, about baptism and about the destruction of pictures in the churches. In regard to the destruction of pictures he, Luther, has done a more thorough job with his writings than Carlstadt ever did with his hands. To destroy pictures is no sin. However, what Luther does object to is that Carlstadt makes a new law of external requirements, binding the consciences of so many people. Then Luther makes the famous statement:

> I must confess to you that if Dr. Carlstadt or someone else had told me five years ago that there is nothing else but bread and wine in the sacrament, he would have done me a great service. I have suffered so many temptations, and have twisted and turned in order to escape this difficulty, since I saw very clearly that I could have given the Papacy the greatest blow. I have heard from two others who have written much more ably about this than Dr. Carlstadt and who did not torture the words according to their own presumptions. However, I am taken prisoner and cannot escape: the Word is too mighty and it is impossible to let them tear it out of my thoughts with other words.[60]

He concludes the letter by encouraging the Strassburgers to stand firm in love and in the Word, to be concerned about the essentials of the Christian faith, and to look neither to Carlstadt nor to Luther, but to Christ for leadership, and to continue the work which they had begun in Christ.

Although no one knew it at this time, Carlstadt's arrival in Strassburg in the fall of 1524 and the correspondence which issued between Strassburg

---

[59] W. A. XV, 391-397.
[60] W. A. XV, 394, lines 12-20.

and Wittenberg, then Strassburg and Zürich, marked the beginning of both controversies over the Lord's Supper which would set group against group and even divide those of the same household. Luther did not really understand that the Strassburg letter was a desperate cry for help. Conditioned as he was by his bitter, personal controversy with Carlstadt, most recently in Jena and earlier in Wittenberg, the word that burned with fiery letters across the Strassburg communication was the name CARLSTADT. He really did not answer their plea for help but rather attacked Carlstadt. A few weeks later, with the full realization of the change which had taken place, namely, that Carlstadt, the Zwinglians, and by guilt of association Bucer and the Strassburg preachers, were now on the opposing side, he wrote the attack on Carlstadt, *Wider die himmlischen Propheten*.[61] Shortly after the receipt of Luther's letter, on December 26, 1524, Bucer published *Grund und Ursach*. In this important writing, contrary to Bucer's own statement that he is faithfully interpreting Luther, Bucer, in his interpretation of the Eucharist, has already moved away from Luther and in the direction of Zwingli.

In the development of Bucer's doctrine of the Lord's Supper four clearly defined stages may be distinguished.[62] The first may be called "the Lutheran stage," for in it Bucer was most strongly influenced by the teaching of "the early Luther." However, as a result of Carlstadt's visit to Strassburg in the fall of 1524, the Strassburg preachers became uncertain about their understanding of the Lord's Supper[63] and it was during this period of indecision that Bucer published *Grund und Ursach*. In the second stage, 1525-1536, Bucer enthusiastically undertook to bring about a union of the Lutherans and the South Germans on the basis of the concept *unio sacramentalis* which he had discovered in Luther's *Vom Abendmahl Christi* (1528)[64] The Witten-

---

[61] W. A. XVIII, 203ff.
[62] W. P. Stephens, in *The Holy Spirit in the Theology of Martin Bucer* Cambridge University Press, Cambridge, 1970, p. 238, mentions the following four stages: (1) 1523-25, (2) 1526-30, (3) 1530-39. (4) 1540-51.
[63] W. A. Br. III, 382, lines 30-34.
[64] W. A. XXVI, 261ff.

berg Concord of 1536 climaxed his efforts. The fourth stage, 1536-1551, showed further developments in his eucharistic doctrine.[65]

Bucer, realizing the futility of attempting to bring about any kind of agreement with the Swiss, withdrew from sacramental discussions altogether. An uneasy peace, broken by Luther's publication of the "Short Confession" of 1544,[66] reigned between the contending parties. During this period Bucer, remaining true to his word given to Luther at Wittenberg,[67] was concerned with establishing the independence of the Church from the Council in Strassburg, working out forms of pastoral discipline and church life[68] and introducing the Reformation in Hesse[69] and Cologne. Due to the many demands upon his time and energy, he resigned his pastorate at St. Thomas in 1540, then suffered the disappointment of failure of the negotiations in the "Cologne Reformation"[70] and the Regensburg-Hagenau-Worms Colloquies. He met with the Spanish theologians at Regensburg in 1547 and at the request of the Emperor was intimately involved in the pre- Interim discussions. His most conspicuous success was the introduction of the Reformation in Philip's Hessen, where many of his proposals which had been rejected by the Strassburg *Rat* were actually put into practice. In 1548 Bucer published *Ein Summarischer Begriff* in which he summarized the faith he had held over the previous twenty years. During his exile in England he wrote *Censura* and *De Regno Christi*,[71] through which, to some extent, he influenced the liturgical, religious, social and political life of England.

---

[65] *Cf.* W. P. Stephens, *op. cit.*, pp. 257-259.
[66] W. A. LVI, 41ff.
[67] Namely, to accept the formula agreed to in the Wittenberg Concord of 1536.
[68] *E.g.*, *Von der waren Seelsorge* (1538), D. S. VII, pp. 90-241.
[69] *E.g.*, *Ziegenhainer Zuchtordnung* (1539), D. S. VII, pp. 260-277 and *Kasseler Kirchenordnung* (1539), D. S. VII, pp. 279-318.
[70] *Einfältiges Verdencken*, carefully analyzed by Mechtild Kohn, *Martin Bucers Entwurfeinere Reformation den Erzstiften Köln*, Luther-Verlag, Witten, 1966. For other writings during this period *cf.* Eells, op. cit., pp. 357-371.
[71] Vol. XV of *Martini Buceri Opera Latina* (Paris, 1955), translated by Wilhelm Pauck, *Melanchthon and Bucer*, Philadelphia, 1969, Vol. XIX of The Library of Christian Classics.

The Lutheran Stage: The concern of the present investigation is limited to the first stage, prior to and immediately following the publication of *Grund und Ursach* on December 26, 1524. In this treatise Bucer claims to follow Luther's teaching in regard to the Lord's Supper[72] and in the letter to Luther of November 23, 1524 he and the other signators obviously look upon Luther as one who teaches them, one whom they follow and one whose advice they seek, especially in the uncertainty with regard to the sacraments in which they found themselves as a result of Carlstadt's teaching.[73]

To what extent was Bucer a "Lutheran" during this stage? The answer lies in examination of Bucer's earliest 1523 writings: *Das Ym Selbs*,[74] *Summary*,[75] and *Dass Luthers Leer*.[76] A careful examination of Bucer's Writings of the year 1523 reveals that he read avidly, studied conscientiously and knew intimately the writings of Luther.[77] In the basic Reformation teachings of the young Luther, Bucer was his uncritical follower. In "*Das Ym Selbs*," Bucer's dependence upon Luther is clear not only in the title itself (taken from "*Freiheit*") and the division into two parts, but also in his basic emphases: the importance of the Scriptures, of faith, of justification and of the priesthood of all believers. His teaching on the secular authorities diverges from Luther's in insisting that they should be responsible for the introduction

---

[72] *Grund und Ursach*, par. 113, p. 162.
[73] Letter of the Strassburg preachers to Luther, W.A., BR. III, p. 381, lines 1-3 (They address Luther as *charissime pater*); p. 382, lines 25-27, (*tecum...hucusque praedicavimus*); and the conclusion, p. 387, lines 226-250.
[74] The full title is *Das ym selbs niemant, sonder anderen lebensoll, und wie der mensch dahyn kummen moeg*, (henceforth *Das Ym Selbs*).
[75] Full title, *Martin Butzers an ein christlichen Rath und Gemeynder statt Weissenburg Summary seiner Predig daselbst gethon*, (henceforth *Summary*).
[76] Full title, "Dass D. Luthers und seiner nachfollger leer...christlich und gerecht ist...", (henceforth *Dass Luthers eer*).
[77] The most important of these would be, among others: *Sermon vom Sacrament des heiligen Leichnams Christi* 1519, W. A. II, 743ff, (henceforth *Sermon 1519*); *Sermon von dem neuen Testament, das ist von der heiligen Messe*, 1520, W. A. VI, 363ff, (henceforth *Sermon 1520*); the three 1520 charters of the Reformation: (l) *De Captivitate Babylonica ecclesiae praeludium* W. A. VI, 497ff, (henceforth *Captivitate*); (2) *Von der Freiheit eines Christenmenschen*, W. A. VII, 20ff, (henceforth *Freiheit*); (3) *An den christlichen Adel deutscher Nation*, W. A. VI, 404.ff, (henceforth *Adel*). Also *Vom Anbeten des heiligen Leichnams Christi*, W.A. XI, 431ff, (henceforth *Anbeten*).

and supervision of the Reformation. True faith leads to true love and issues in good works to the glory of God and the well-being of the neighbor.[78]

A different emphasis in the interpretation of justification by faith is evident. Whereas Luther interprets faith in "psychological-pedagogical categories,"[79] Bucer's emphasis is expressed in practical-ethical categories. The *Summary* restates in theological form and content the substance of "*Das Ym Selbs.*" Again the treatise rests upon the basic Lutheran principles of *sola scriptura* and *sola fide*.[80] Where he does not follow Luther (the opposition of flesh and spirit, that the doing and not doctrine or dogma are basic aspects of the Christian man), he follows Erasmus.[81] The *Summary* was written to encourage the congregation at Weissenburg to stand firm in the evangelical convictions which he had taught them, and further to prove to the Strassburg *Rat* that his teaching and preaching in Weissenburg had been truly orthodox.[82] In the first two articles of *Summary* he states his basic theological position, first, the Word of God is the only norm, and second, Christ is the only redeemer.

Article V deals with the mass.[83] Even before coming to Strassburg Bucer had called the Mass *nachtmal Christi*. The Lord's Supper is to remind us of our sins and to comfort us by the remembrance of the sacrifice of Christ but in no way a sacrifice itself. The purpose and benefit of the sacrament should be to make us hate the world and the flesh, to increase our love for God and our neighbor, to strengthen our faith and love and comfort us in all our tribulations. Vestments, mass gestures and all accouterments of the Roman Mass are to be abolished. The language used should be German.

The most systematic exposition of Bucer's faith showing his agreement with Luther's teaching is found in *Dass Luther's Leer*.[84] Although Luther is

---

[78] D. S. I, pp. 66-67.
[79] D. S. II, pp. 32-40 and the valuable footnotes on these pages.
[80] He uses extensively Luther's 1519 *Galatian Commentary, Adel,* and *Captivitate.*
[81] D. S. I, pp. 77.
[82] *I.e.,* in harmony with evangelical principles.
[83] D. S. I, 117ff.
[84] *Cf.* p. 26, note 5. This treatise was published for the first time in D. S. I, pp. 310–344. The original manuscript by Bucer has not title, date or signature. The date Oct./Nov. 1523 is established in D. S. I, pp. 304–308. The contents agree in substance with the "Summary."

mentioned only twice, at the beginning and at the end, Bucer, using Luther's writings,[85] makes his first and most important point that it is the Holy Scriptures which are the basic authority for the Christian. To this authority he relates justification, the priesthood of all believers, the secular authorities and the mass. In regard to the sacraments, he gives a detailed description of all seven Roman Catholic sacraments and on scriptural grounds retains only two. On the same grounds he rejects purgatory, monastic vows and the worship of saints and the Virgin Mary.[86] The mass, as in the *Summary*, is called *nachtmal Christi*. The remembrance of the death of Christ brings about the hatred of sin, the denial of the world and the flesh, the strengthening of patience to bear our trials, the willingness to love God and serve our neighbor.[87] The mass is defined as "the remembrance of the eternal sacrifice of Christ on the cross offered for us."[88] In the bread and the wine we receive the body and the blood of Jesus Christ.[89] All externals added to the mass which have no basis in Scripture and which hinder faith and love, must be rejected.[90]

A basic shift in Bucer's interpretation of the Lord's Supper took place in the fall of 1524 when John 6:63 and the commemorative aspect of the Lord's Supper became prominent in his writing.[91] In a letter to Zwingli on December 31, 1524,[92] Capito states that Bucer has accepted "with heart and soul" Zwingli's interpretation of the Eucharist whereas previously leaned more in the direction of Luther's teachings.[93] Bucer, in a letter to Martin (Frecht)[94] describes the three events which brought about this change. The first of

---

[85] Bucer uses *Captiviate* twice as often as all the other writings of Luther. The next most often used is *Freiheit*.
[86] D. S. I, pp. 332-339.
[87] *Ibid.*, p. 330.
[88] *Ibid.*, p. 331, lines 17-19.
[89] D. S. I, p. 330.
[90] *Ibid.*, p. 350.
[91] E.g. *Handel mit Cunrat Treger,* October 20, 1524, D. S. II, pp. 37-173, especially pp. 72, 61, 109, 119. Note Bucer's estimate of Treger in W. A. Br. III, 386, lines 191-206.
[92] J. W. Baum, *Capito und Butzer*, pp. 300-303.
[93] *Ibid.*, p. 302, lines 19-21.
[94] *Ibid.*, pp. 303-305. Editor's note: Martin Frecht was a noted Reformer in Ulm who was present at the Heidelberg disputation with Luther, Bucer, and others notable Reformers.

these events was the appearance of Carlstadt in Strassburg. Although he only stayed four days, everyone in Strassburg became aware of his teaching through the distribution, avid perusal and vigorous discussion of some of his seven writings on the Lord's Supper. The content of his sacramental teaching was summarized in the letter of the Strassburg preachers to Luther and in Carlstadt's *Dialogus*.

In an attempt to find a satisfactory answer to the questions raised by Carlstadt's writings, Bucer listed on a piece of paper the relevant passages in the gospels and in Paul, to discover whether Carlstadt's interpretation was scriptural. His conclusion was that Carlstadt's position was questionable and unscriptural.[95] He expressed the result of his own study in the following way:

> As in baptism mere water is used, so also in the Lord's Supper is mere bread. They are each mere symbols, and you may add to the bread what you will, and change it into whatever you will; it will still remain only a sign, and even an unnecessary sign if you are not lifted up, through faith, to Christ who has died for you and sits at the right hand of the Father and at the same time dwells in you. If this happens, you have no time to contemplate the physical presence, which is of no use to you in any case.[96]

He states that it was John 6:63 which brought him to this conviction. In regard to his dependence on Luther in the past he states that no one ever admired Luther more than he, but goes on to say, "This sort of admiration is conducive to putting blinders on spiritual vision."[97]

The Enigma of Carlstadt: One of the haunting and perplexing problems of Reformation research is the enigma of the personality of Andreas Carlstadt. Luther's judgment of him as a spiritualist, destroyer of pictures and anar-

---

[95] J. W. Baum, *op. cit.*, pp. 303-304.
[96] *Ibid.*, p. 304, lines 3-10.
[97] *Ibid.*, p. 305, lines 13-15. *Cf.* this assertion with *Grund und Ursach* par. 113, p. 162.

chistic agitator has colored the understanding and interpretation of his life. Denominational prejudice has depicted him as a villain, without making any real attempt to investigate the facts of his life. Like Bucer's, Carlstadt's works were forgotten and buried in the vitriolic judgment of Luther as given in his tracts during the time of the sacramental controversies. Some extensive accounts of his life have been written. One of these shows the hue of Lutheran dislike of the man,[98] the other attempting and for the most part succeeding in the attempt to be fair to him.[99] It is only recently that Gordon Rupp has tried to depict him as he was in the context of the Reformation as a whole.[100] But the definitive life of Carlstadt is still to be written.

Carlstadt was neither a villain nor a fool. His writings are the products of a scholarly, trained mind. When Luther came to Wittenberg, Carlstadt occupied the superior academic and ecclesiastical positions. He was elected dean of the theological faculty several times. His biblical studies broke ground in many areas,[101] and Luther indirectly paid respect to his scholarly findings when he accepted Carlstadt's judgment as to the Epistle of James.[102] He had written a respectable study on Augustine.[103] His writings on the Lord's Supper were treated with respect, albeit with some reservations, by many biblical scholars of his day.[104] The deliberate and single-minded persecution by Luther, which followed and sometimes even preceded Carlstadt wherever he went; his abject poverty for a great part of his life; his forsaking high positions in the academic world to become a simple layman-farmer in order to identify with the common people; his involvement with Muntzer and the Peasants' Revolt; his escape from Rothenburg

---

[98] C. F. Jäger, *Andreas Bodenstein von Carlstadt,* Stuttgart, 1856.
[99] H. Barge, *Andreas Bodenstein von Karlstadt,* 2 vols., Leipzig, 1905.
[100] G. Rupp, *Patterns of Reformation,* Philadelphia, 1969, pp. 49-153. *Cf.* also the perceptive article, *Andreas Bodenstein of Carlstadt* by Hans J. Hillerbrand in *Church History,* December 1966, pp.379-398; and further: George H. Williams, *The Radical Reformation,* Philadelphia, 1962, especially pp. 38-44, 68-75, 100-103.
[101] Barge, *op. cit.,* I p. 293f, p. 304, 411; pp. 186ff;II pp. 79ff.
[102] *Ibid.,* I, p. 197f.
[103] Ernst Kähler, *Der Kommentar des Andreas Bodenstein von Karlstadt zu Augustins Schrift 'De spiritu et litera'.* Halle, 1952.
[104] His numerous sacramental treatises, and the positive results of the *touto* controversies.

in the midst of a violent peasant upheaval by being let down, secretly, over the city wall—all these and many more happenings in his colorful life would make a most exciting scenario for a super-spectacular movie, or supply the inspiration for authors of novels and plays.

There was indeed a fatal flaw in his character which was responsible for most of his woes. He was a self-seeking opportunist many a time; he often betrayed the trust of friends; he was not always too careful in money matters. Zwingli hit the nail right on the head when he said of Carlstadt that he "is easily offended and offends easily."[105] On the other hand, he was a successful and beloved pastor at Orlamünde. So radical and far-reaching were his liturgical reforms in Orlamünde, so well-informed were his parishioners, so great and wide-ranging was his circle of friends and followers, that for a while—just for a little while—it seemed possible that Orlamünde might become a third important Reformation center. It was not to be. Constantly on the move, hounded by dislike, pursued by distrust, struck down by hatreds, he finally settled down in Basel. With the best wishes and recommendations of his Strassburg friends, he would spend the remainder of his life (from 1534 to 1541) in the town to which Erasmus had retired and there, in the midst of a busy life as a preacher and a professor at the University, on Christmas Day in 1541 the plague claimed Carlstadt as one of its victims.[106]

On April 14, 1534, in a letter to his friend Myconius, Bullinger's appraisal of Carlstadt is very revealing: "You need not fear that he Carlstadt is the kind of person Luther describes. He is most cooperative, modest and humble, and in every respect above reproach."[107] Even in death he found no peace. All sorts of ghost stories about him made their appearance. For many a German youngster he became "that which frightens children into being good"[108] and the unrelenting hatred of Luther, and the fully justifiable but

---

[105] *Karlstadt erscheint uns ein solcher der leicht beleidige undbeleidigt werden kann;* as quoted in Barge, *op. cit.,* p. 278.
[106] For a brief account of Carlstad's life and work *cf.* Hertzsch, *op. cit.,* pp. x-xxiv.
[107] As quoted in Hertzsch, *op. cit.,* p. xvi.
[108] *Cf.* Barge, *op. cit.,* Exkurs VIII, Karlstadts Nachleben, vol. II, pp. 510ff.

vicious spleen of his own wife, followed him beyond the grave.[109] Why should Luther have attacked him so virulently in *Wider die himmlischen Propheten,* by claiming that the effects of his teaching and his actions on the common, simple and trusting people who had been committed to his care were the same as those of murder and revolt? Why should Luther spend so much time and energy, not to speak of paper and ink, in refuting Carlstadt's exegesis of *touto* and ridicule him for his "*tutten und tatten*" while condemning him with biting irony for his spiritual self-righteousness, his sophistry and his reliance on "Frau Hulda"? There are, to be sure, all the obvious answers and explanations based, on personal, scholastic and theological differences between these two men. In this particular situation, however, explanations will have to go beyond the obvious. The relationship between these two would make a fascinating and fruitful study for both normal and abnormal psychologists.

The second factor responsible for the shift in Bucer's interpretation of the Lord's Supper is found in Hinne Rode's visit[110] to Strassburg in November, 1524. Rode must have been a persuasive and attractive personality[111] and he brought with him a letter written by Cornelius Hoen (Honius) which was to have decisive influence upon Bucer and later upon Zwingli. While cataloguing the library of a friend, Hoen had come across Wessel Gansfort's *On the Sacrament of the Eucharist.* So deeply was he impressed by this book that he reinterpreted his own thinking on the Lord's Supper in the light of Gansfort's position. Then he published his findings in *Epistola Christiani admodum*,[112] in which, rejecting transubstantiation, he says:

> Nor indeed did the Apostles speak of the sacrament in this fashion;[113] they broke bread, and they called it bread; no Word about this Roman belief. Nor is this contradicted by St. Paul, who, although he says, "The

---

[109] *Ibid.,* pp. 515ff.
[110] He left Strassburg on November 21st.
[111] D. S. I:189. On Hoen, *cf.* also G.H. Williams, *op. cit.* pp. 33-37 85-89.
[112] Now translated in full in Heiko A. Oberman, *Forerunners of the Reformation,* N.Y. 1966, pp. 268-276.
[113] *I.e.,* that Christ is in the bread.

bread which we break, is it not a participation in the Body of Christ?" does not say that the bread is the Body of Christ. It is therefore obvious that in this text "is" *(est)* should be interpreted as meaning "signifies" *(significat)*.[114]

After discussing the three kinds of spiritual bread: "Christ, Who is eaten by faith, as John says, the *manna* which the fathers ate in the desert, and the Christian Eucharist," he continues: "Thus the Eucharist is neither a living bread nor a bread of life." Discussing the famous passages in John he says that "St. John refers not the eating by mouth but by faith."[115] After attacking the ritual of the Mass and the teaching of the Roman Church, he concludes:

Let us distinguish, therefore, between the bread received by mouth and Christ, Who is received by faith. But if anyone does not discern the Body of the Lord, thinking that he has eaten nothing more than what he took by mouth, he is answerable to the Body and Blood of the Lord, and he eats and drinks his own judgment, he shows Christ to be present while he separates himself from Christ by his own unfaith.[116]

A group of humanists in the Netherlands felt that this *Epistola* would help Luther in his conflict with the Roman Eucharist teaching and help him to formulate his own. They sent Hinne Rode to take it to Luther.[117] Rode arrived in Wittenberg in 1521, when Luther's own affairs were in a very confused and critical state. Luther rejected Hoen's interpretation.

Hinne Rode, who was the rector of a school in Utrecht, was dismissed from his position upon his return because of his contact with Luther.[118] Hoen himself was arrested as a "Sacramentarian,"[119] and was forbidden to

---

[114] Oberman, *op. cit.,* p. 269.
[115] Oberman, *op. cit.,* p.273.
[116] *Ibid.,* p.276.
[117] *Cf.* The introductory remarks and notes, Oberman, *op. cit.,* pp.252-255; also George H. Williams, *op.cit.,* pp.27-37.
[118] *Propter Lutherum.*
[119] For definition, *cf.* C.H. Williams, *op. cit.,* pp. 27-28.

leave The Hague, where he had been a lawyer at the court. Soon afterward, in 1524, he died. Hinne Rode, on his journeys as an eõcile, still bearing the *Epistola,* arrived in Strassburg on his way to Zürich. In his letter to Martin (Frecht) Bucer describes the visit of Rode, who was his house guest and left on November 21,[120] two days before the Strassburg preachers sent their letter to Luther. Bucer describes how, Scripture in hand, he had defended Luther's position with all his might and then makes the significant statement; "But then I realized that, with all my arguments, I was unable to hold my own against this man's conviction, and that it was impossible to prove from the Scriptures that which I wished to believe. I was forced to reject the physical presence of Christ in the bread, even though I was somewhat uncertain about the true explanation of the words."[121]

The third decisive factor in the development of Bucer's doctrine of the sacraments was the teaching of Zwingli. When the Strassburg commotion forced the preachers to take a stand on the questions raised among the people by Carlstadt, they sent communications both to Luther and to Zwingli, asking for advice and guidance from both. Zwingli's reply was accompanied by a copy of a secret letter which he had sent on November 18 to Matthaeus Alber, minister in Reutlingen, who in the dispute between Luther's and Carlstadt's positions planned to defend the position of Luther.[122] Zwingli, trying to dissuade him from doing so, wrote this lengthy letter clarifying his own position. Bucer, writing to (Frecht), states that he has received communications from Zwingli in which Zwingli explained to him privately that which soon would become public knowledge. Bucer confesses that as a result of these communications Luther's interpretation now seems very weak to him.[123] The importance of Zwingli's letter to Alber lies in the fact that it states succinctly the basic elements of Zwingli's sacramental teaching. One of these is the element of commemoration. He says, "The

---

[120] This date is established in the letter of the Strassburg preachers to Luther, W. A. , Br. III, 386, line 216.
[121] J. W. Baum, *op. cit.*, p. 305, lines 6-10.
[122] Walch, Vol. XVII, cols. 1512-1529; *Cf.* 3, 340-341.
[123] J. W. Baum, *op. cit.*, p. 303.

Lord's Supper has been instituted for this purpose, that we should think of the death of Christ, which he suffered for us." This commemoration should lead to a joyful thanksgiving, expressing itself in an act of public confession of the church's unity and a pledge *(Eid)* of communion with Christ and with one another. An expression of this feeling of communion should be a sincere faith and an unblemished Christian life. Christ's food is the gospel, that is, that he died for us on the cross. Another basic aspect of Zwingli's teaching is his interpretation of John 6:63. In another publication[124] he says:

> I recognize the sixth chapter of the Gospel of John as the most effective means in the battle. There lies the priceless jewel, 'The flesh is of no use.'… In the second instance it seemed to us that the most important was John 1:18: 'No one has seen God.' Here the worship of everything which is visible and physical is forbidden.[125]

These three factors, involving Carlstadt, Hinne Rode and Zwingli, were responsible for Bucer's change in emphasis, away from Luther and in the direction of Zwingli. None of the participants in this drama seem to have been aware that decisive differences of interpretation on the Lord's Supper would divide Protestantism. Luther was the one most sure of his position, but even he did not yet know that he himself would be so affected by the events transpiring at this time that he would enter another stage in his own development, namely opposition to Zwingli, and his own single-minded, stubborn espousal of the real bodily presence of Christ in the bread and wine, together with his violent opposition to any "spiritualistic," subjective interpretations of the Lord's Supper.[126]

Köhler claims,[127] and rightly so, that the publication of Zwingli's letter to Matthaeus Alber in March, 1525, in Zürich marks the real beginning of the great battle over the true interpretation of the Lord's Supper. Luther in a

---

[124] *De vera et falsa religione commentarium,* March 1525.
[125] Z III, p. 270.
[126] *Cf.* P. Althaus, *The Theology of Luther,* Philadelphia, 1966, pp. 375-376.
[127] W. Köhler, *Das Religionsgesprach zu Marburg 1529,* Tübingen, 1929, p. 14.

letter to Spalatin in October, 1525, informs him that "the Strassburg preachers have sent a messenger with many letters in which they desire that we agree with them on the Zwinglian teachings concerning the Lord's Supper."[128] The messenger referred to was Gregorius Casel, professor of Hebrew in Strassburg, whom the Strassburgers had sent to Luther, urging him to moderate his fierce public disapproval of Zwingli and Oecolampadius. Luther sent Casel back with a brief reply but gave him detailed instructions for the Strassburgers.[129] These include attacks on Zwingli and Oecolampadius and show his exasperation with the Zwinglians' arrogant claim to the certainty of their salvation. To Luther it indicates that they do not feel deeply enough and do not think deeply enough about these matters. He rejects the interpretation of *est* as meaning *significat* and accuses them of torturing the Word of God and misleading the people. "For in this matter," he says, "we deal with that which is of the greatest danger to salvation. If, then, they are fully convinced that they are right and do not want to or cannot desist, then we must compare this whole sorry affair with the frantic upheavals at the time of Arius," and he underlines: "But they shall not conquer."[130]

The Meaning of the Lord's Supper

Bucer, like the other Reformers, opposed the Roman Catholic doctrines of transubstantiation, the sacrifice of the Mass, and the practice of distributing the elements in one kind. He agreed with them that this act of worship is a divine institution commemorating the death of Christ. He, too, believed in the presence of Christ in the elements and considered it to be the highest act of worship because it expressed union of the worshippers with Christ and with one another, with special blessings for those who participate worthily. The differences among the various interpretations concerned the mode of Christ's presence and the organ and extent of reception. By 1525 Luther recognized the teaching of Zwingli as being opposed to his and applied to it

---

[128] W. A., Br. III, p. 593.
[129] W. A., Br. III, pp. 604-606. *cf.* also *ibid.*, pp. 606-611.
[130] Walch XVII, col. 1538.

the word "Zwinglian."[131] Whereas in the Lutheran interpretation the emphasis was on the Word, in the Zwinglian it was on faith. The differences in sacramental interpretation were determined by differences in the doctrine of God and in their Christology. The Lutheran emphasis was on the interpenetration of the divine and human, and leaned towards Eutychian Christology; the Zwinglian was on the sharp separation of the divine and the human and leaned toward the Nestorian Christology. As a result, there were divergent emphases in the different conceptions of the relationship between church and state, God's work and Christ's, forms of worship, and piety.

Lutheran piety was marked by mystical overtones, the Zwinglian by practical, "psychological pedagogical categories."[132] The strange discrepancy between Bucer's judgment of Luther as found in *Grund und Ursach* and the November 23 letter to Luther on the one hand, where he speaks in terms of regard and dependence, and in the letter to Martin (Frecht) on the other hand, where he expresses a complete rejection of Luther's teaching, seems paradoxical. However, one explanation might well be that at this stage of his development Bucer was neither a Lutheran nor a Zwinglian. By background, intellectual training and temperament, that is, as a Christian humanist, he naturally would incline more to the teaching of Zwingli than that of Luther. What was to become his outstanding trait, namely the function of mediator, the ability to adapt, harmonize and utilize two opposing points of view, is already discernible. In regard to the doctrine of the Lord's Supper, this special ability of Bucer was later to find its fruition in the sacramental teaching of Calvin.

Bucer's doctrine of the Lord's Supper as it emerges in *Grund und Ursach* can be stated in several propositions.[133] The first of these is that the Lord's Supper is *not a sacrifice*. Bucer's polemic against this doctrine is vigorous

---

[131] In his letter to Spalatin, October 30, 1525. W.A., Br. III. 593.
[132] D. S. I, p.39.
[133] W. P. Stephens (*op. cit.*, p. 238, footnote 1) states that Bucer's primary concerns during this period (1523-1525) were "chiefly the issues of flesh and Spirit, spiritual enjoyment, and remembrance."

and uncompromising. True to his first basic principle, everything which is contrary to the Word of God must go. The teaching of the Roman Church on sacrifice is contrary to the Word of God. It is a "most abominable abomination,"[134] "it is a remembrance and in no way a sacrifice."[135] He has a horror of the sacrifice and of the sacrificers.[136] It is a blasphemy, because the priests presume to sacrifice Christ and handle God.[137] It is a "horrid and corrupt error"[138] and therefore the name must be changed. It is no longer a mass but a *Nachtmal des Herrn*.[139] The practices in connection with the Mass are not only unscriptural but they are pagan and idolatrous practices and inventions of the human mind. For this reason the Canon and the elevation must be abolished.[140] The only sacrifice acceptable to God is the sacrifice of ourselves.[141]

In the second place, *the Lord's Supper is a memorial*.[142] Luther's concept of *testamentum* as an anniversary should logically have led to the interpretation of the Lord's Supper as a memorial.[143] However, as a result of his exegesis of the *verba*, Luther never went in that direction. Due to the influence of Zwingli, Hoen and to some extent Carlstadt, but primarily because he felt that this was the best way to understand the Lord's Supper, Bucer constantly emphasizes the memorial aspect of the Supper. "The Lord's Supper is a memorial and a thanksgiving for our salvation, through which faith in God is strengthened and love to all men is rekindled and refreshed, but first of all to the members of the household of faith."[144] This statement might almost serve as Bucer's definition of the Lord's Supper, although other elements were added to it. "The Lord's Supper is nothing but a remembrance

---

[134] *Grund und Ursach*, par. 9.
[135] *Ibid.*, par. 42; also par. 53.
[136] *Ibid.*, par. 9.
[137] *Ibid.*, par. 63.
[138] *Ibid.*, par. 73.
[139] *Ibid.*, ch. II.
[140] *Grund und Ursach*, ch.IV.
[141] *Grund und Ursach*, par. 28; *cf.* also par. 1; par. 27.
[142] *Ibid.*, the entire ch.III.
[143] In the 1520 "Sermon"; he evades the whole problem in *Vom Anbeten* (1523).
[144] *Grund und Ursach*, par. 100.

of such a sacrifice."[145] The content of that remembrance is the saving death of Christ. There was only one sacrifice and it was "once-for all."[146] When refuting Carlstadt's exegesis of *touto*[147] he speaks of the Lord's Supper as a remembrance. There should be no quarrel about words, since we have the clear command of Christ when He told us to remember Him. Remembrance and proclamation are quite often paired together. In the exhortation in the Sunday Liturgy, remembrance occupies a prominent place.[148] To Bucer, anamnesis was an important aspect of his doctrine of the Lord's Supper.

A third point, closely connected to the preceding aspect, was the emphasis on *eucharistia*. Here again he was indebted to Luther's 1519 Treatise[149] in which the grateful, worshipping congregation, the Church which is Christ's spiritual body, gives thanks to God for His great love. This was also an important aspect of Zwingli's understanding of the Lord's Supper. Bucer feels very strongly that the Lord's Supper should be observed with praise and thanksgiving. We should come together "to proclaim, to praise and to glorify the death of Christ for our salvation, and become like Him."[150] "In the Lord's Supper we should think with faith and thanksgiving of His death and of His sacrifice, that He sacrificed Himself to the Father once and for all on the cross for the sins of the elect."[151] In another passage which recalls the note of glad celebration of Luther's 1519 and 1520 treatises,[152] Bucer says, in speaking about the Lord's Supper, that it is our sacrifice of praise and thanksgiving and that we should recall at that time "the sacrifice which was offered once-for-all for us and which has eternal validity. In doing so we proclaim the Lord's death, give Him the praise and glory and encourage

---

[145] *Grund und Ursach*, par. 27.
[146] *Ibid., par. 39 (also par. 17, 18, 19); par. 24.*
[147] *Ibid., par. 107; par. 109.*
[148] *Ibid., par. 95.*
[149] The judgment of Brilioth: "The rediscovery of the idea of communion is the greatest positive contribution of the Reformation in regard to the eucharist; it is of more value than all the criticisms of the mass," *op. cit.,* p. 97.
[150] *Grund und Ursach*, par. 104.
[151] *Ibid., par. 24.*
[152] Luther's 1519 and 1520 *Sermons*.

one another in love and good deeds, since we are one bread and one body in Christ."[153]

A further element of Bucer's teaching on the Lord's Supper is *synaxis*.[154] It has been recognized that Luther, in this aspect of his teaching in the 1519 treatise,[155] came closest to the spirit of the primitive church. In his understanding of the Lord's Supper as *communio,* or fellowship, and of *communicare* as participation by members of a worshipping congregation, he reached depths of the real significance of the Supper which unfortunately he was to lose in the controversies with the Roman Church and the "spiritualists." To Bucer *synaxis* was a very important emphasis in the worship of the church and in this he acknowledged his indebtedness to Zwingli. "The Lord's Supper is a bond of Christian community through which we, like Christ, that is through Him and for His sake, have all things in common."[156] "The Lord's Supper should never be observed for one person alone, but should be observed by all disciples of Christ in the congregation.[157] For this reason it should be observed on Sundays only,[158] so that the whole congregation can worship together and recall together that we are "sinners together, damned together, saved together"[159] through the death of Christ. Christ belongs to all and through Him all have true communion of the body and blood of Christ, and all are one body and one bread. Together they observe the memorial of His death and thanksgiving, and together their faith is strengthened and their love refreshed. Citing the example of the custom of the Ancient Church,[160] he spends all of chapter VIII to provide a fitting vehicle for the common worship of the church.

---

[153] *Grund und Ursach*, par. 28.
[154] Most of ch. VIII, *Grund und Ursach* , deals with community through communion.
[155] English translation of this significant treatise is found in *Works of Martin Luther,* The Philadelphia Edition, Philadelphia, 1943, pp. 9-31.
[156] *Grund und Ursach*, par. 84.
[157] *Ibid.*, par. 85.
[158] *Ibid.*, ch. VII.
[159] *Grund und Ursach,* par. 85.
[160] *Ibid.*, par. 89.

Another underlying idea of Bucer's doctrine of the Lord's Supper is that of "eating the flesh and drinking the blood of Christ spiritually."[161] Like Zwingli, Bucer had been influenced by the teaching of Nominalism, with its separation of spirit and flesh. John 6:63 became for Bucer, as it was for Zwingli, the distinctive emphasis.[162] "Whatever is physical will be of no help to you; if, however, you should accept the spiritual, it would bring you eternal life." [163] "Accept both of them (the bread and the cup) as right and true; be concerned only with this, that what you receive, you receive in memory of the Lord, so that you through faith receive the flesh and blood of Christ spiritually, that is, believe without any reservation whatsoever that through such a sacrifice you have been made a child of God. Anything else we need to know, God will surely reveal to us."[164] *Summa Summarum:*

> Hold fast to the words of the Lord and do not do violence to them; but remember all the while that the flesh is useless and that everything which is physical here refers to the spiritual. The Lord commands you to eat and to drink: that is physical; but the sole purpose is that you should think of Him, believe Him, thank Him and be obedient to Him, Who gave His body and His blood for you.[165]

These moving words, which reveal the warmth and depth of Bucer's piety and incorporate so fully the Zwinglian attitude to the Lord's Supper,

---

[161] *Ibid.*, par. 103; *cf.* Also: "spiritually and truly," par. 107; "spiritual partaking of the flesh and blood of Christ," par. 116; "spiritual eating and drinking," par. 142. Stephens, *op cit.*, p.242, after remarking on the ambiguity of the word "spiritual," during this stage of Bucer's sacramental development, sums up Bucer's position by saying that "Bucer's understanding of the sacrament is that the bread and wine are in themselves flesh, without Spirit, that they should lead to a remembering of the saving death of Christ which is the source of Christian faith and life, and that this remembrance in faith, together with the physical eating and drinking, is equivalent to a spiritual enjoyment of the body and blood of Christ" (p.245).
[162] Stephens, *op. cit.*, p. 242, suggests that "John 6:68 may be said to view the sacrament rather from the godward side, and John 4:23-24 from the human side".
[163] *Grund und Ursach*, par. 111; *cf.* also paragraphs 104 and 112.
[164] *Ibid.*, par 112.
[165] *Ibid.*, par. 113.

must have seemed strange to Luther when he read them and surely must have indicated to him that Bucer, contrary to his claims, was no longer fully on his side.[166]

Closely connected with the preceding is a further aspect of Bucer's interpretation of the Lord's Supper, namely that *the Lord's Supper is a sign and a symbol*. Again the influence of Zwingli is quite obvious. Here is also one of Bucer's governing ideas, the radical separation of flesh and spirit, spirit and nature. "There is however, never any holiness in things themselves."[167] "In our time a special power has been ascribed to the sign."[168] As a result a great deal of superstition has grown up in regard to the understanding of the Mass, and that which the sign signifies, namely the death of Christ, has been ignored. "We should not overemphasize the sign and reject its significance, or prefer the shadow to the reality," for then "the knowledge and the power of Christ are nullified."

Throughout *Grund und Ursach* Bucer's main concern is his fear of assigning too much significance to the external observance of the sacraments. Ceremonies are a mark of the Old Testament and are contrary to the spirit and also contrary to the worship of God in spirit and in truth.[169] At one point[170] he cautiously observes that many[171] consider the Lord's Supper to be an external matter which by itself is not essential. However his basic attitude to the externals of the sacraments shines forth in the oft-repeated: "Signs are signs and should remain signs, and it should in no way be admitted that the signs are what they signify."[172] Outward signs are merely vehicles of grace,

---

[166] For the later development of Bucer's doctrine, *cf.* Cyril C. Richardson, *op. cit.*, pp.24, 37-38. W. P. Stephens, *op. cit.*, p.245, states that the "gaps" in Bucer's doctrine which were to be filled in later are: "The presence of Christ (and in particular, the manner of his presence) in or with the elements, the understanding of the sacraments as a communion between Christ and the Christian, the role of the Spirit in making the death of Christ a present reality, and the relation of the sacrament to Christ's intention in instituting it."
[167] *Grund und Ursach,* par. 64.
[168] *Ibid.,* par. 80.
[169] *Ibid.*, par. 75, 77.
[170] *Ibid.*, par. 89.
[171] Note the use of the word "many," as though he were excluding himself from their number.
[172] *Ibid.,* par. 79.

and just as God does not limit his grace to water, which in baptism is nothing in itself,[173] neither is His grace limited to bread and wine as such. The spiritual remembrance,[174] the spiritual eating and drinking, that is, eating and drinking in faith,[175] offer us the benefits. In words which echo Hoen's *Epistola* he says: "You have heard Christ say, 'the flesh is of no use'; why then do you ask about the flesh? If you could recognize it as a symbol and a sign and accept it with true faith that He gave and sacrificed His body and blood on the cross once for all for your salvation; then you would truly partake of the true body and the true blood of Christ and have eternal life."[176] One of the benefits won for us through a spiritual remembrance of the once for all death of Christ on the cross[177] and the spiritual eating and enjoyment of the flesh and blood of Christ by faith,[178] is the forgiveness of sins. "If we believe without any doubt whatsoever that He died for us, then this salvation is offered to us: we have been delivered from evil and become children of God."[179] The true meaning of "to sacrifice" is this, that: "in it the once for all sacrifice of Christ is remembered which, if it is accepted in faith, will bring the fruit of the sacrifice of Christ, namely the forgiveness of sins and all mercies."[180]

Other benefits of the Lord's Supper are eternal life, and sonship.[181] When Bucer speaks about the benefits of baptism, in addition to mentioning as benefits the forgiveness of our sins, eternal life[182] and the bestowal of sonship,[183] he also mentions the gift of the Holy Spirit,[184] which is given to the elect, those who believe in Christ. Rebuking Carlstadt, Bucer says that Carlstadt "should be more concerned about why the sacraments were insti-

---

[173] *Ibid.*, par. 128.
[174] *Ibid.*, par. 55, 57.
[175] *Ibid.*, par. 142.
[176] *Grund und Ursach,* par. 24, 111, 112.
[177] *Ibid.*, par. 55, 57.
[178] *Ibid.*, par. 112.
[179] *Ibid.*, par. 111, 112.
[180] *Ibid.*, par. 27.
[181] *Ibid.*, par. 111, 112.
[182] *Grund und Ursach,* par. 12.0, 121, 124, 126.
[183] *Ibid.*, par. 139.
[184] *Ibid.*, par. 121, 126.

tuted rather than what they are in themselves."[185] He underlines his position by saying that all that matters is that we wholly believe that through Christ's sacrifice we are rescued from sin and become children of God. "Anything else God will reveal."[186] The *results* of the Lord's Supper as expressed in *Grund und Ursach* are outlined in some of the most eloquent and moving passages of the book. Here his pastoral concern as the leader of a congregation and the shepherd of his "lambs" shines through and finds expression in the *Doppelgebot:* his characteristic emphasis upon the pairing of *fides et caritas.* A typical passage, which reflects many of those appearing in *Grund und Ursach,* is the following: "The Lord's Supper is a memorial and a thanksgiving for our salvation, through which faith in God is strengthened and love to all men is rekindled and refreshed."[187]

As a result of participation in the Lord's Supper there will be a right attitude within the individual and a right relationship within the community. In a person's own life faith is strengthened, *i.e.* he has the certainty and assurance that his sins and all evils are forgiven, and that in this life salvation and eternal life, through the death of Christ, are his. The believing individual becomes like Christ by dying to sin, by carrying his cross manually and by showing a sincere love to all. In his relationships to the community, as a result of his participation in the Lord's Supper the Christian should spend himself in love and service for the neighbor. True Christian love even demands that, if the necessity arises, he should be prepared to die for the good of the neighbor. Here we find one of the underlying emphases in *Grund und Ursach*. Luther in his *Invocavit* sermons, Carlstadt in his sermon on the great commandment, and Zwingli in his emphasis on the Lord's Supper as a *Gemeinschaftsmahl* which joyfully expresses the bond of uniting love, demanding evidence in a life of mutual service, are no more eloquent and no more insistent than Bucer upon the ethical requirements of Christian *agape.* Bucer regrets that the Lord's Supper, which should be the expression of the greatest unity among Christians, should have become the occasion for the great-

---

[185] *Ibid.*, par. 112.
[186] *Ibid.*, par. 100.
[187] *Ibid.*, par. 85.

est splits and hatreds. He reproves Carlstadt for causing discord by quarreling over words,[188] and he reproves all those who, exalting secondary matters, forget that which is essential, namely the expression of faith and love and service and unity. Consequently there is his constantly repeated demand, that everything which is contrary to the Word of God and which harms right faith and true love and unity must be overcome and abolished, so that the true Christian witness may illumine the world. Finally, the manner of observing the Lord's Supper was of great concern to Bucer.[189] Most of *Grund und Ursach* is the attempt to justify the reform measures undertaken in Strassburg, so necessary because of the many abuses which had arisen in the church. "The mass vestments are not only lying and vainly deceiving inventions, leading to much superstition and error, and have been most harmful and disadvantageous to the purity of the faith, but they have also successfully prevented brotherly love and almsgiving to the poor, and have in addition encouraged ostentation and pride.[190]

Passages like these are found over and over again in *Grund und Ursach*. Not only are vestments attacked, but all those external customs, observances and superstitions which had adhered to the Mass during the centuries. Bucer's ideal was a return to biblical simplicity, but primarily an emphasis upon reality in worship. He condemns superstition and sham, but even more so the princes and priests of the church, who grow fat at the expense of the poor and simple masses. He again applies a basic principle here: everything which is not in harmony with the Word of God and which harms faith and love must go. Worship must be in spirit and in truth, and its main purpose is to strengthen faith and rekindle love.

All adornments and embellishments are inventions of the human imagination and come from the devil. *Adiaphora* are secondary and, in the observance of some ceremonies and the abolition of others, Bucer makes an amazing number of concessions for the sake of the weaker brethren. You cannot win their souls if they have been frightened away. Concerning

---

[188] *Grund und Ursach,* par. 9, also par. 99; par. 118; par. 142.
[189] *Cf.* section entitled *The Shape of the Liturgy,* below, pp. 266ff.
[190] *Grund und Ursach,* par. 65.

things indifferent,[191] the religious leaders must "distinguish carefully the circumstances of all ordinances in order to differentiate between the temporal and the eternal."[192] Since all external adornments in worship belong to the temporal and not to the eternal order,[193] and since the weight of tradition hangs very heavily on most of them, "it is difficult to keep the right proportion."[194] However, keeping in mind constantly the demands of the Word of God and by acting in harmony with the principle of faith and love, the elect have the responsibility to make sure that their words and their deeds agree, and the preachers, in addition, have the responsibility of extensive and careful teaching and preaching, with the hope that in the end the reforms will be accepted and furthered. One of the outstanding liturgical scholars of the Reformation claims that, liturgically, *Grund und Ursach* is one of the most important documents to come out of the Reformation era.[195] A careful examination of the shape of the liturgy is therefore of great importance. Beforehand, however, Bucer's doctrine of the second sacrament which he accepted as valid, namely the sacrament of Baptism, needs to be considered briefly.[196]

Baptism

In his earliest writing Bucer does not consider Baptism important enough to spend a single word on it; in his second publication he grants it only a few words. In *Grund und Ursach,* however, an entire chapter[197] is devoted to this subject. It is difficult to escape the impression that even here his treatment is *pro forma* rather than a matter of deep urgency. The take-it-or-leave-it tone contrasts strongly with the remainder of the treatise. The biblical arguments and justifications are the weakest in the whole writing, and he leaves no one

---

[191] *Grund und Ursach,* par. 44.
[192] *Ibid.,* par. 46.
[193] *Ibid.,* par. 72.
[194] *Ibid.,* par. 47.
[195] Smend, *op. cit.,* p. 147.
[196] W. P. Stephens, *op. cit.,* pp.221-228, states that no significant changes took place in Bucer's doctrine of Baptism as found in writings between 1523 and 1530. With regard to the teaching of the "radical reformers" on Baptism, *cf.* G. H. Williams, *op. cit.,* pp.300-319.
[197] Chapter IX.

in doubt that baptism with water is definitely not a means of grace. However, with the coming of the first few refugees to the hospitable "city of righteousness," soon to flood it with all kinds of problems for the preachers and magistrates, questions about baptism were to become of major concern. In 1524 Bucer was forced to take a position because of the appearance of Carlstadt, who rejected infant baptism. Further, Baptism was one of the two sacraments which Bucer had accepted as being biblical. He describes as one of the most significant reforms undertaken in Strassburg, in connection with Baptism, that:

> we teach through the Word that external baptism is a sign of the true baptism of Christ, that is of inner purification, rebirth and renewal; through which they should consider themselves and others honored and held in high regard as those who are Christ's and will receive such an inner new birth; and that the cleansing from sin and the renewal of disposition are due to Christ alone, Who through His Spirit cleanses, gives faith and saves the elect.[198]

Bucer distinguishes between two kinds of baptism: baptism with water and baptism with the Holy Spirit. The former is the baptism of John, of all the apostles and of the preachers in Strassburg. This external baptism with water is nothing but a symbol,[199] and is the outward sign of the inner and spiritual baptism.[200] Since the outer baptism with water is a "thing indifferent," it should certainly not be denied to the children who are members of the household of faith. External baptism will not save, and to say that unbaptized children will be lost is to shame and belittle the death of Christ. "God does not limit His mercy to water,"[201] and "we cannot limit Him to time or place."[202] Bucer's justification of infant baptism rests on the fact that

---

[198] *Grund und Ursach*, par. 130
[199] *Ibid.*, par. 126.
[200] *Ibid.*, par. 124.
[201] *Ibid.*, par. 128.
[202] *Ibid.*, par. 138.

in apostolic times whole households, including children, were baptized by the apostles.

He finds it most difficult, for pastoral reasons, to reply to the injunction that instruction and believing should precede baptism. To quarrel over words here, since it is a dispute over non-essentials,[203] will destroy the peace, unity and growth of the congregation and will hinder both faith and love. Therefore, "why make such a fuss over a lot of water?"[204] The important baptism is the baptism with fire and Holy Spirit, which is Christ's baptism. The benefits of this baptism are inner purification, rebirth and renewal. It is Christ's baptism alone which cleanses, gives faith to and saves the elect.[205] "Without the Spirit, water is only water, and will not save."[206] The reforms which have been undertaken in Strassburg with regard to baptism are, first, that people are properly instructed with respect to the meaning of baptism, and second, that all previous superstitious practices and customs have been abolished. Bucer then gives a description of the simple service which is being used in Strassburg.[207] Baptism is not only a comfort to the parents, who know that their children are incorporated into the body of Christ, but parents and god-parents taken upon themselves the obligation to love the children and to make sure that at the proper time they are instructed as to the meaning and significance of their baptism.[208] No one had any idea at this time that this simple instruction would in a few years lead to the important development of the idea of confirmation. Bucer, to a large extent, was the father of this concept.

The Shape of the Strassburg Liturgy

The most striking phenomenon in a study of the Strassburg Liturgy is the realization that in an amazingly short time, namely between February, 1524 and December of the same year, a radical change has taken place in liturgy.

---

[203] *Ibid.*, par. 142.
[204] *Ibid.*, par. 140.
[205] *Ibid.*, par. 120.
[206] *Ibid.*, par. 127.
[207] *Ibid.*, par. 132.
[208] *Grund und Ursach,* par. 132.

On February 16[209] Theobald Schwartz, Zell's assistant at the cathedral, celebrated the first German Mass in the Laurentian Chapel of the cathedral, and a few days later Anton Firm at St. Thomas read the second Mass in German. Immediately the Strassburg citizens expressed the desire to have their children baptized in German and to receive the elements in both kinds. The episcopal vicar, Dr. J. Odernheim, protested to the *Rat* against this change. A disputation with the Protestant preachers was proposed but never held, and the Mass in the German language became the norm.

Schwartz's Mass was so popular that it was printed and reprinted several times. Basically is was the Roman Mass according to the customary Strassburg rite as observed between 1513 and 1520 but translated into German with minor, yet very significant, changes. All references to the Mass as a sacrifice were removed. The Mass was said in German in a loud voice (so that all could hear), the elements were distributed in both kinds to those who so desired, but there was neither sermon nor song. When this conservative service is compared with that described by Bucer in *Grund und Ursach*[210] and in the letter of the Strassburg preachers to Luther on November 23, the radical simplicity of the service is truly astonishing. The priest is called *Diener*, the altar has become a table and is placed so that all in the church can see the minister. The service is conducted from behind the table. The minister delivers a brief explanation of the Lord's Supper, the Gospels are read, from Matthew, Mark and Luke, along with 1 Corinthians 11, the elements are distributed in both kinds, the minister partaking last of all. The stark simplicity is relieved by another astonishing innovation: the singing of hymns. In *Grund und Ursach* the congregation sings four times: a psalm at the beginning and one at the end of the service, the Decalogue is sung before the sermon, and the Apostles' Creed after it.

---

[209] A detailed, historical description of this first Mass was published by J. Smend, outstanding liturgical expert, at Strassburg, 1897, entitled *Der erste evangelische Gottesdienst in Strassburg,* an address which he delivered to the Protestants of Strassburg on March 16, 1897. *Cf.* also Smend, Julius, *Die evangelischen deutschen Messen bis Luthers deutsche Messe,* Göttingen, 1896, (henceforth, Smend).
[210] Par. 95.

We are most fortunate in having an eyewitness account of the services in Strassburg as given by Lefevre d'Etaple's student, Gerard Roussell. Both had arrived at Strassburg in the early weeks of 1525 as exiles from Meaux and were Capito's house guests. It is interesting to set this eyewitness account alongside Bucer's description and to see how closely they correspond.

A table is set in the cathedral in such a way that it can be seen by all. They do not call it an 'altar' in order to avoid all resemblance to those who have made a sacrifice of the supper. The table, however, does not differ at all from ordinary altars. The minister approaches it in such a way that his face and not his back is turned to the people---while all eyes are fixed on him, he reads several prayers taken from the Scriptures, and they are short prayers. Next everyone sings a psalm. After this the minister, having prayed again, mounts the pulpit and first reads the Scriptures, which he explains in a manner understood by all. After the sermon the minister returns to the table. Everyone sings the creed. Then an explanation is given to the people of the benefit of the supper which Christ has given us. During the communion everyone partakes of the supper and sings the *Kyrie Eleison* to render thanks for the benefits received. The minister partakes last of all and finishes what remains. After that each one goes to his house and returns to the cathedral after dinner, around noon, to hear the sermon which one of the pastors addresses to the people.[211]

It is quite obvious that when Bucer says in *Grund und Ursach* "we have abolished" and "we have changed," he means just that. Roussell is particularly struck by three things in the service of worship, first, that the images have been removed from the churches and all that remains is "the sole worship of God according to the clear and pure Word of God"; and second, by

---

[211] Doumergue, E., *Essai sur l'histoire du culte reforme principalement au XVI et au XIX siecle*, pp. 8,9. Libraire Fischenbacher, Paris 1890. *Cf.* also the letter of the Strassburg preachers to Luther dated Nov. 23, 1524 which states in substance what Bucer describes at greater length in *Grund und Ursach*.

"the singing of the women mingling with that of the men (which) produces a ravishing effect;" and third, that "although there were a considerable number of services, there was not one of them which was not frequented by a large crowd."[212]

A question which arises immediately is: What, if any, was Carlstadt's influence on these radical changes? He had, to be sure, come to Strassburg with a radical teaching. His radical actions in Wittenberg and later in Orlamünde might lead us to the conclusion that he would be in the forefront of radical action wherever he happened to be. However, we know that on his first visit to Strassburg he did not even make a courtesy call on the Strassburg preachers. As a matter of fact, one of their complaints against him was that, as a result of Carlstadt's activities in the city, attendance at the regular services of worship was declining. Besides, at this time the preachers did not think too highly of his word-splitting and "quarrels over words," nor of him as a person, so that any suggestion of influence from his direction is quite out of order.

Another question which may be asked is: What influence may Luther have exerted in effecting the Strassburg innovations? Luther's repudiation and quick action to correct what in his judgment was the "harm" done by Carlstadt in Wittenberg, indicate that Luther himself would hardly approve of the liturgical "experimentation" taking place in Strassburg. Further, his own liturgical reforms were slow in coming[213] and were the result of outside pressures. It was Bugenhagen, over the objections of Luther, who in 1542 abolished the elevation in Wittenberg. Luther's reluctance to initiate sudden reforms must be explained by his inherent conservatism. More than any of the other Reformers, he was a child of the medieval thought world. His love for the church and its ritual, his dread of violence and the use of force, either external or internal, in matters not only of politics but also of faith and conscience, would never countenance radical change. One of the points of difference between him and Carlstadt had been just this. To the

---

[212] Doumergue, *op, cit.*, p. 8.
[213] The *Deutsche Mess und Ordnung* was not published until 1526.

question: Should one go slowly in implementing changes? Luther and Bucer would answer in the affirmative. Luther does so in his Advocavit Sermons, and Bucer does so, over and over again, in *Grund und Ursach*. Carlstadt's answer was given in print for everyone to read.[214] Would a parent allow a child to play with a sharp and dangerous knife? Of course not; he would remove the knife, even over the child's objections. Besides, God's commandments must be obeyed, regardless of the weaker brethren. The harm done to them spiritually by making weak concessions would be far worse than the effects of ruthless abolition of harmful customary practices. Any influence Luther might have had on the Strassburg reform would be through his writings. That influence, however, was theological rather than liturgical.

The earliest reforms in the liturgies simply meant the translation of the Latin Mass into the vernacular and the omission of the Canon. That of Kaspar Kantz of Nordlingen in 1522, printed in Strassburg, had extensive sections of the Mass in German. A far more radical reform was undertaken in 1523 in Allstedt by Thomas Müntzer. It is only recently that the liturgical genius of Müntzer is being recognized. The beauty, liturgical excellence, evangelical warmth and musical appeal, in many respects superior to those demonstrated by Bucer, are now being appreciated. [215]

The most radical reform of worship, of course, had taken place in Zürich under Zwingli's leadership. The *Second Zürich Disputation* of October 26, 1523, dealt primarily with the mass and with images. The Council, desiring to proceed gently in implementing such radical changes, chose to wait until the people were properly instructed. Zwingli, in his *Short Christian Introduction*, written in November 1523, hoped to prepare the people of Zürich for the reform, which would during the following year transform the interiors of the churches by removing all the trappings of the Mass, so that almost

---

[214] *Ob man gemach faren tmd des ergernüssen der schwachen verschonen soll,* published in Basel, Nov. 1524; in E. Hertzsch No. IV; also discussed in *Rupp, op. cit.,* p. 138.
[215] *Cf.* the sympathetic interpretation in Rupp, *op. cit.,* Part III, pp. 157-353, especially Ch. 20, pp. 305-323.

nothing but white walls would remain.[216] Bucer approved of the manner in which this reform was accomplished and the procedures employed by the governing authorities in Zürich because reform was accomplished decently and in order.[217] Zürich became his model. It is quite obvious, then, that radical changes and creative experimentation and expressions were in the air. Consequently the radical nature of the Strassburg reforms was not as unusual as it might seem at first sight. The energy, drive and enthusiasm of Bucer in this, as in other matters, would be explanation enough. The significance of the Strassburg reform was the whole-hearted and enthusiastic support of the worshipping community. Bucer was the driving force behind these efforts. It is not difficult to imagine him as the chairman and leader of seminars on worship with the rest of the preachers. Capito's letter[218] reflects so closely the teaching of *Grund und Ursach* that he must have been well instructed by Bucer — and all of the preachers signed their names to *Grund und Ursach*. A closer examination of the shape of Bucer's Liturgy might be in order. Through Calvin, who lived in Strassburg from 1538 to 1541, ministering to the French congregation there, the Strassburg Liturgy was to become the mother of a number of Reformed liturgies throughout the World.[219] Calvin himself acknowledged his debt to Strassburg by saying: "As for the Sunday Service, I took the Strassburg form and borrowed the greater part from it."[220] The structural outline of the liturgy as described in *Grund und Ursach*[221] and in the Strassburg letter to Luther is as follows[222]:

Confession and Absolution
Psalm or Gloria sung by the congregation
Collect

---

[216] Grimm, H. J. *The Reformation Era*, N. Y. 1954, p.187.
[217] *Mit Fug und Stille, Grund und Ursach* , par. 162.
[218] *Was man halten und antworten soll von der Spaltung zwischen Martin Luther und Andreas Carlstadt* (Autumn, 1524), Walch XX: 340-351.
[219] *Cf.* Cypris, O. F., *Public Worship in Calvin,* unpublished dissertation, 1953, pp. 51-101.
[220] From the farewell address delivered on April 28, 1564; *Opera Calvini* IX:894.
[221] *Grund und Ursach*, par. 95.
[222] The letter of Nov. 23, 1525; Walch XV:2055-2065.

Epistle with exposition
Decalogue sung by the congregation
Gospel
Sermon
Credo sung by the congregation
Common prayer of intercession
    For those in authority
    For all people
    For those present
Lord's Supper: exhortation
    Words of institution
    Distribution
Hymn of Praise
Prayer and Benediction

None of the known Strassburg liturgies exactly fits this outline. The closest to it is *Des Herren Nachtmal*.[223] Schwarz's German Mass was printed at least four times during 1524.[224] All are still called the "German Mass." By the early part of 1525 Bucer's influence becomes evident. The Strassburg liturgies are marked by progressive simplification and application of evangelical principles. Now they are no longer called "Mass," but *Des Herren Nachtmal*. By 1529 all masses in Strassburg had been abolished by action of the *Rat*, and from 1526 to 1539 still further reductions and further trends toward simplification can be observed.[225] Although in the beginning Bucer had looked upon spontaneity in worship and the expression of the freedom of the spirit as an ideal, by 1534 he began his efforts toward uniformity. Nonetheless, from the very beginning some orderly form had been prescribed, as is evident from the many liturgies which were printed, but it

---

[223] Smend, *op. cit.*, p. 155f, feels that D1 and D2 come closest. Smend describes *Grund und Ursach* as "without any doubt, the most important basic writing in matters of liturgy, which was produced by the Reformation." p. 147.
[224] These are listed as A1, A2, A3, A4 and described in detail. Smend, *op. cit.*, pp. 125-138.
[225] Smend, *op. cit.*, pp. 152-155.

seemed to Bucer that liberty was becoming license. He no doubt was reacting to his experience with the Anabaptists and the various "spiritualistic" groups.

With his deepening clarification of the concept of the meaning of the church,[226] and the necessity of bearing a united witness to unity in Christ, Bucer felt that some measure of uniformity was desirable. The description of the liturgy as we find it in *Grund und Ursach* and reflected to a large extent in the "D" liturgies can be summarized as follows: The name "Mass" is changed to "The Lord's Supper."[227] All references to the Canon and to the Lord's Supper as a sacrifice are removed.[228] The celebrant is no longer a "priest" but a *Diener*.[229] The elevation, which in Wittenberg was retained until 1542, is abolished.[230] A simple table replaces the altar.[231] A simple choir gown is worn by the celebrant instead of the elaborate vestments of the Mass.[232] So sure is Bucer that these vestments will become unfamiliar and forgotten relics that he describes them in some detail, for the benefit of posterity![233]

The Lord's Supper is observed only on Sundays,[234] so that the community can participate. There are only two sacraments. In the Lord's Supper "those who so desire" may receive the elements in both kinds.[235] Holy days are abolished, because they have given rise to many excesses and immoralities.[236] All pictures and images are abolished, because they encourage dependence on superstition rather than on God, and hence nullify the death of Christ and blaspheme God, as well as fill the pockets of avaricious priests.[237] Emphasizing reality in worship, he declares that all worship

---

[226] Cf. J. Courvoisier, *La Notion d'Eglise chez Bucer,* Paris, 1933, pp. 50-62.
[227] *Grund und Ursach*, ch. 2.
[228] *Ibid.*, ch. 3.
[229] *Ibid.*, ch. 3.
[230] *Ibid.*, ch. 3.
[231] *Ibid.*, ch. 4; par. 83.
[232] *Ibid., ch.* 5.
[233] *Ibid.*, par. 59.
[234] *Grund und Ursach*, ch. 7.
[235] *Ibid.*, ch. 8.
[236] *Ibid.*, ch. 10.
[237] *Ibid.*, ch. 11.

should be spiritual worship, in spirit and in truth.[238] By the end of the year 1525, singing had become an established and popular part of the service.[239]

During the early Schwarz Masses there was no singing, although Luther's hymn, *Gott sei gelobt,* seems to have been recited. In the *Teutsch Kirchenampt* of 1525 most of their hymns have musical notation. The music for some of these was supplied by Wolfgang Dachstein, assistant and organist at St. Thomas, and Matthaeus Greyter, assistant at St. Stephen's and "singer" in the cathedral.[240] *Grund und Ursach* provides for the singing of hymns in four places in the service, and for the brief vesper services provision is made for two or three psalms, one of these to be sung before and one after the sermon. The impression of joy and thanksgiving seems to have permeated these services, which were well attended by the citizens.[241] Bucer felt strongly that songs and prayers should come spontaneously from the heart, should be voiced "with the spirit," should be in the vernacular, and should be based on the Scriptures alone.[242] In the beginning he made use of materials already at hand, as, for example, some of Luther's hymns, but by his insistence upon the Scriptures as the only true source of hymns, Bucer became the father of Calvinistic and Puritan psaltery. Here then lies the beginning of the contrast between the Reformed and the Lutheran approach to worship and music.[243] In the end the Lutheran approach served to enrich hymnody and gave rise to the masterpieces of Bach and others.

Prayers, too, are to be spontaneous and in the vernacular[244] and are to replace the prayers in the Mass, since the latter have encouraged superstition and a disdain for the divine Word of truth. God, being spirit, is to be worshipped in spirit and in truth. An interesting feature is the offering of prayers not only for those present and for all people, but also for "those in authority." Bucer's hope that the Strassburg *Rat* and the Protestant minis-

---

[238] *Ibid.,* par. 69.
[239] *Cf.* the impression made on Roussell.
[240] Adam, *op. cit.,* p. 71.
[241] Gerard Roussell's description, *supra,* p. 100.
[242] In harmony with the first and most important of his principles.
[243] *Cf.* H. Davies, *The Worship of the English Puritans,* Glasgow, 1948, ch.II, pp. 13-24.
[244] *Grund und Ursach,* par. 179-185.

ters would share the secular and ecclesiastical responsibilities equally, and that in spiritual matters the spiritual leaders would give direction to the secular leaders was disappointed. The *Rat*, anxious to prevent the old domination by the church, was reluctant to surrender its authority over both secular and spiritual affairs. Near the end of his life Bucer had to come to terms with this situation and solved the problem by his teaching on the church as an *ecclesiola in ecclesia*. More than a hundred years later, Jacob Spener, to his great surprise, was to discover this concept in Bucer, and to adapt it to those private devotional house gatherings known as *collegia pietatis*.[245]

Bucer's attitude to *adiaphora*, which includes all externals of the liturgy: vestments, images, holy days and even the sacraments of Baptism and the Lord's Supper, is expressed as follows: "Signs are signs and should remain signs, and it should in no way be admitted that the signs are what they signify."[246] If signs become what they signify, they become hypocrisy, and hypocrisy is harmful because, first, it is blasphemy to use, handle and slander God and knowledge, and the death of Christ, which has set us free from bondage to external things, is nullified thereby. Hypocrisy is harmful secondly, because consciences are bound and superstitions multiplied, and thus, thirdly, love is harmed, especially so if the priests exploit the superstitions of the common people. Therefore, superstitions customs and practices must be abolished (even though at times for the sake of the weaker brethren they may be retained, provided there is proper and lengthy preaching and instruction which will lead to their eventual abolition). They must be abolished because they are contrary to the Word of God, and that is reason enough for their removal, but even more so because they are against faith and love: against faith because they encourage reliance upon things rather than God; against love, because the poor suffer. The money is wasted on superstitious practices and customs rather than given to the poor. Quite obviously Bucer, arguing from different premises, always arrives at the same

---

[245] *Cf.* in this connection *Puritanismus und Pietismus,* August Lang, Neukirchen 1941.
[246] *Grund und Ursach,* par. 79, par. 80, par. 109, and par. 140 (re Baptism).

conclusion; the love for the neighbor, which is an exposition of his characteristic *Doppelgebot*.

Many of the *adiaphora* are retained for a while and are abolished slowly without noise and tumult, through the agency of the authorities, but only after the people have been thoroughly instructed through preaching and teaching. This general method is applied to the vestments. The masquerade and mummery of priestly vestments led to ostentation, pride and exploitation of the common people. The origin of the vestments is found in pagan customs and human inventions contrary to the Word of God. Since we are all priests, our vestments should be truth, justice and righteousness. We should put on Christ, reject all pride and ostentation, and surrender our bodies to God, which is a true sacrifice of praise and thanksgiving. Our best spiritual adornments are true faith and true love. The only vestment used by the Strassburg preachers is a simple choir gown.[247] In a similar way images are abolished. Roussell notices with amazement the absence of images and "of nearly all which men have added to the worship of God."[248] Bucer himself mentions that the *Rat*, following the example of Zürich, has removed some images, idols and pictures from the churches quietly and without fuss.[249] In Bucer's church, St. Aurelian, the congregation removed the tomb and covered up the vault of St. Aurelia, which had become an object of worship, pilgrimage and idolatrous superstition. "Bones are bones," says Bucer, "they are not God." It is God alone Who should be worshipped.[250]

Bucer's pastoral concern for the spiritual wellbeing of the Strassburger is most apparent in his insistence that all holy days except Sunday should be abolished, because of the immorality, superstitions and gross excesses in connection with the celebration of these days.[251] He insists that they be abol-

---

[247] *Grund und Ursach*, ch. 5.
[248] Doumergue, *op. cit.*, p.9.
[249] *Grund und Ursach*, par. 162.
[250] *Ibid.*, par. 174-178.
[251] *Grund und Ursach,* par. 147. The constant refrain is, "One day is as good as another" and God should be worshipped every day. Bucer paints a vivid picture of the immoralities current in Strassburg.

ished immediately. No concessions to the "weaker brethren" here! He who would try to please the people and win their favor by being tolerant would only indicate that he fears people more than God.[252] Brotherly love and pastoral concern for all includes even the servants, who need one day of rest and Worship in seven. A special service was held in Strassburg for the servants and the children over whom the servants must keep watch while their elders were at worship.[253] Sunday should be a day of worship, of creative rest and Christian service for all. When Bucer later attempted to enforce the observance of Sunday, the *Rat* demurred. Bucer reproved the members of the *Rat* who should, but did not, set an example of sabbath observance.

Bucer's attempts to reform the liturgy and the external observances are cause for the greatest admiration of the man who, single-handed and with singleness of mind and purpose, attempted to make Strassburg a miniature of the Kingdom of God on earth. The basic principles which underlie *Grund und Ursach* were applied with fidelity and determination. All of them could be summed up in the following: *Ein Christ hat nur zwei Grundsätze, nach denen all sein Thun und Lassen sich richtet: die Ehre Gottes und die Liebe des Nächsten. Beides zu erfüllen hat er nur eine Lehrerin und Regel: die Heilige Schrift in ihren klaren und hellen Aussprtichen.... Was ihnen zuwider ist muss weichen und fallen.*[254]

---

[252] When it comes to abolishing holy days, Bucer follows Carlstadt rather than Luther! One of the most eloquent passages in all of *Grund und Ursach* is par. 151, which describes the abuse of holy days.

[253] *Cf.* Cypris, *op. cit.*, pp. 43-44.

[254] G. J. Van de Poll, *Martin Bucer's Liturgical Ideas,* Assen, 1954, p. 15, footnote 5. Translation from German to English: "A Christian has but two foundational principles that shape all his doings: The honor of God and the love of neighbor. To fulfill both, he has only one Teacher and standard: the Holy Scriptures in their clear and bright sayings. Whatever contradicts them must yield and fall."

Martin Bucer's Ground and Reason

A Translation

By

Ottomar Frederick Cypris

Contents

Covering Letter (*Sendschreiben*)   73

I. Concerning the Innovations in the Lord's Supper   87

II. Concerning the Name of the Lord's Supper   91

III. That the Lord's Supper Should Be Held as a Memorial of the Death of Our Lord and in no Way as a Sacrifice   93

IV. Reason for Abolishing the Elevation   102

V. Reason Why the Popish Vestments Have Been Abolished   118

VI. Why the Prayers and the Gestures Used by the Priests Have Been Abolished and Changed, and Further, Why the Table Called Altar Has Been Displaced   126

VII. Why the Lord's Supper is Held Only on Sundays in the Presence of the Congregation   133

VIII. The Manner in Which the Lord's Supper is Observed Now   139

IX. Concerning Baptism   149

X. Why We Have Abolished Holy Days   159

XI. The Reason Why Images Should Be Abolished   169

XII. Why Songs and Prayers in the Church Have Been Changed   176

Covering Letter
(*Sendschreiben*)

To His Serene Highness and Illustrious Prince and Lord, Friedrich Count Palatine by the Rhine, Duke of Bavaria, My Most Gracious Lord.

1

Your Serene Highness, Illustrious Prince, Gracious Lord. Mercy and Peace of God the Father and of the Lord Jesus Christ be to Your Excellency with the offer of my humble and willing service, always ready at all times heretofore and now. I give thanks and praise to God, our merciful and most gracious Father, who so mercifully has protected Your Excellency that you have in no way been influenced to persecute the Gospel of Our Savior Jesus Christ, in spite of the fact that some of the so-called spiritual leaders have attempted to do so with all their might, but instead has granted you a receptive heart inclined to His Holy Word,[1] the evidence of which can be seen day by day and more and more in true Christian acts. For it is an especially great mercy and blessing of God if He puts godly princes in authority over us, just as it is an expression of His great anger and heavy judgment if He gives great authority to the godless, children and fools, and it can be read in many other places in the Scriptures, such as in the prophet Isaiah 3:32. And the wise Prince Solomon says: "When the righteous flourish, it is well with the people, but when the godless rule, the people mourn" (Pro. 29:2). Therefore, along with all the faithful it is an especially great joy to me in the Lord that I hear praise, as to how Your Excellency, along with some other princes, is inclined to further the Holy Gospel—which is a visible, wholesome reflection of His pity and great mercy—in which I have rejoiced on behalf of Your Excellency in a very special way. For you have received and kept me most graciously as your servant after I had been set free from the monastery

---

[1] All scriptural references in the original manuscript of *Grund und Ursach* list chapters only. In this translation, following D. S., verse references are added.

wherein, indeed, there are very few who know God, and after God led me into another vocation you let me go with your consent and permission so that I naturally desired Your Excellency's wellbeing and health, above any other thing, and have prayed for them with the greatest diligence to Almighty God, and have noticed with great thanksgiving and delight in my heart that He has granted you these richly. May He, our God and Lord, who holds the hearts of all kings and princes in His hand (Pro. 21:1), and who alone works in all both the desire and the deed (Phil. 2:13), grant that His work be begun, continued and completed in you, namely the knowledge of His most beloved Son, our Lord Jesus Christ: "Whom He has resurrected from the dead and set on His right hand in heavenly things, over all princes, power, might, rule and all things which could be named, not only in this world but also in the world to come; and has put all things under His feet, and has placed Him above all things as the Head of the Church, which is His body, and the fullness of Him who fulfills all in all" (Eph. 1:20–23).

2

It cannot fail, as the Lord Himself has prophesied, that there must be many, who appear under His Name and will spare no possible effort among many, but primarily among princes and lords, since many depend on these, to turn them away from this our Savior to other matters and inventions as is their custom. "Surely it would be futile to spread a net in the sight of a bird," as Solomon says in Proverbs 1:17. The Lord Himself, who makes wise the simple, gives this certain assurance to Your Excellency that you have inspired and directed the eternal Word of God in such a way that those deceivers have been unable to succeed in their deception and false hypocrisy. For there is no one, unless he has been rejected and blinded by God, who would not see immediately from the clear Law of God that, according to our actions, we are altogether sinners and are condemned, and not a single person can be found anywhere on earth who is able to love God with his whole heart and his neighbor as himself; on which two commandments hang the whole Law and the Prophets, so that he who fails in these breaks all the commandments of God. Since, then, all of us break these divine commandments and for this reason are damned and accursed, we are not able to free either ourselves or other people from such condemnation and curse; as long as we remain in such disfavor, all our actions are unacceptable to God. If the tree is rotten, how can it bear good fruit? Since all of God's Scriptures point and lead us to accept that we belong to the only blessed seed of Abraham, in whom all nations are to be blessed, namely to our Lord Jesus Christ, who alone redeems His people from sins and through whom alone we receive, through a true faith, forgiveness of sins and eternal blessings who would dare to be so foolish as to presume that he could receive this by himself or any other creature, his own or some other's work, be it confession, required satisfactions, indulgences, the good deeds of monks, or all the other things which have been invented for the comfort of some lazy-bellies but to the great harm and detriment of the poor, simple souls?

3

Christ says: "Come to me, all you who are weary and heavy laden, and I will refresh you.... No one comes to the Father except through me.... Without me you can do nothing" (Matt. 11:28; John 14:6; 15:5). Who would not want to leave everything and surrender himself completely in full trust and faith? Truly, he who trusts our Lord Jesus Christ in this way and surrenders himself to Him with true faith, such a heart alone can believe and love our Savior, and consequently will surely hate his sins and his whole previous life and will have thorough repentance and dislike of it, and he surely will acknowledge from his heart and confess his sins before God and all men, where it would bring about change for the better, and just cause to turn himself to God's kindness. Repentance will no longer consist of praying the *Pater Noster* one or five times a day, in giving weekly alms once or twice, in fasting annually for one day or six, but in praying always and without ceasing in spirit and in truth, and in calling upon God in his heart for mercy for himself and for all men, and furthermore he will spend all his life soberly, rejecting all physical superabundance, subduing his flesh and being obedient to the Spirit, and surrendering his whole life, what he is and can do, in service to his neighbor and to everyone who is in need of him, and in being prepared to do for everyone what Christ Jesus has done for him, who laid down His body and life for His enemies; and this is truly and indeed a Christian praying, fasting and almsgiving, yes, it is the only true repentance, which every Christian should be prepared to practice his whole life long, and be prepared to suffer and to endure everything which God sends his way. In this way he dies to sin and is perfected in the baptism of Christ, and further considers and shows forth in his own life the death of Christ, and in order to further this remembrance and to strengthen it, he also takes the Lord's Supper, and knows that through his mere presence at the Mass, or through any other meritorious action, he can do nothing against sin or earn any kind of merit. This is what it means to be a true Christian and such fruits are the result of faith wherever he may be; this is taught by all the divine Scriptures, and this is the content of the preaching of those who preach the Word of God and the Gospel; yes, Gracious Lord, this is the unheard of, most harmful, most poisonous heresy which rejects all good laws and order, tears down and destroys obedience, peace and unity and against which our so-called spiritual prelates presume to motivate all princes and lords. Therefore it is fitting that one should take action against them with iron, water and fire, just as one would take action against the Turks and the worst enemies of God who ever appeared on the face of the earth. But such stupidity is nothing new; their predecessors, the Pharisees and the Scribes, did the same thing to Christ our Lord, who preached exactly the same thing and in addition led a most holy life, and more than that, confirmed His actions and His teaching with so many great miracles. And even before this, the same fate befell all the prophets and afterwards all the apostles and all those who have ever taught the truth from the beginning of the world. The world cannot do anything other than to hate and persecute Christ and him who is His disciple.

4

Your Excellency has lived with so many so-called spiritual leaders, prelates, cardinals, bishops and abbots and others, and is acquainted with their ways, but this I know, that you pray to God that He may protect you from this kind of spirituality, which you have observed in most of these same spiritual fathers. Luxury and voluptuousness cannot be found, even amongst the most worldly of the princes, to the extent that it is found among those who are held to be of the highest saintliness and who even require that their feet should be kissed. Now it is true that Christ once said, and it cannot be interpreted in any other way: "Who is not with me," he says, "is against me;" he who does not gather with Him as the wind gathers chaff, yes they are like Him in all things, as water is to fire, as night to day, as hell to heaven. In Christ one beholds nothing but humility and contempt for temporal things, with them nothing but magnificence and pride; in Christ poverty and an inclination to be prepared at all times to help everyone, with them wealth and avarice for which even the earth is not big enough; in Christ there is nothing but complete gentleness and meekness, with them war, murder, condemnation without trial, driving people into exile, burning and destruction; in Christ, constant teaching and preaching, with them gambling and hunting. To sum up, Christ carries His cross at all times so that He can help others, but they allow themselves to be carried in sedan chairs and put the cross on all who do not voluntarily worship them. Christ takes nothing but gives freely to everyone; they take from everyone and give nobody anything for nothing, unless they are beautiful girls and amusing entertainers.

5

It is for this reason, Your Grace, that Christ says so earnestly "Either plant a good tree and it will bear good fruit or plant an evil tree and it will bear evil fruit; for a tree is known by its fruit. You generation of vipers, how can you speak good things while you are evil? for the mouth speaks out of the overflow of the heart. A good man brings forth good things from his good treasure and an evil man brings forth evil out of his evil treasure" (Matt. 12:33–35), and people everywhere can see such fruits in our so-called spiritual leaders and also in those who defend them, who claim to be Christian spiritual fathers like pine cones on aging tree, and so we cannot help but see and proclaim that they are evil trees and consequently their counsels, teaching and ordinances are anti-Christian too: "For the mouth speaks out of the overflow of the heart." Therefore, when they are supposed to advise how Christians should be taught and governed in a Christian way, it is the same as if one desired to set faithful shepherds over the sheep but would ask the advice of wolves. It is plain as daylight and cannot be denied that they do not seek God, for if they did they would live differently; they seek after luxury and voluptuousness; how are they able either to advise or undertake anything that is good?

6

An evidence for this is that they strive so fearfully to prevent matters of our faith and Christian teaching from being debated publicly but all those who do not please them in their preaching are condemned without a hearing. Christ, however, does not lie when He says: "He who does evil hates the light and cannot live in the light; so that his deeds are not punished. But whoever does the truth comes into the light so that his deeds may be made known, for they are done in God" (John 3:20). Indeed they have so many highly learned doctors clothed in velvet and scarlet, that all the institutions of higher learning are full of them; if their cause so just and what we preach so unjust, why then don't they come into the light? The Scriptures of God are written for all the faithful and all the faithful have the Spirit of Christ, through which the Scriptures can be understood: well, then, let them take the Scriptures in hand, and every part will reveal His teaching and His deeds and therefore all Christians will see how much or how little every part is in harmony with the Scriptures. In regard to such a trial and judgment, of course they are unable in any way to accuse Your Excellency and other princes and authorities which they call secular, for surely no one has less understanding concerning these [divine] matters than they, and this is quite evident and no one can deny it; and all the faithful could and should understand, discuss and judge all matters that relate to faith and worship. For God has given His Scriptures only to His faithful, and so all things are judged by those who are spiritual (1 Cor. 2:15); for he who does not have the Spirit of Christ is in no way His (Rom. 8:9). Furthermore, if everybody should believe in God, then everyone must know what is the Word of God, which alone is to be believed. Therefore, just as it is against nature to condemn anyone without a hearing, and since Christ Himself says that all the lambs know His voice, and furthermore, since the old and the most reputable councils were supported by emperors and were held in their presence and the presence of those under their control, Your Excellency should never be persuaded to support those who, without a hearing and with excessive zeal for passing judgment, condemn and destroy all those who do not preach according to the approval of those spiritual leaders referred to, and who do not allow any judge except themselves to function. For it is against all natural inclination to allow Christ to be preached in any other way and to condemn without trial all those who preach Him differently from those who, through all their actions, show that they are the avowed enemies of Christ.[2] It will in no way help them that they constantly assert that our preaching and teaching have been condemned at Constance at the regular Council by all the estates of the Empire, since it is impossible to hold a Council for each one separately; it would be irresponsible to allow another disputation concerning those matters which were decided with due deliberation at the Council. However, Council here, Council there, it is the Word of God that should be preached; if there is anyone who does not preach it and will not desist, he should be killed, but he should be examined first and then tried in order to discover whether he had preached for it or against it. But for that no one needs a Council; every Christian government will be able to recognize, if they have the Word of God, whether their opinion is in harmony with it or not. The contention is not over the legality, concerning what should be preached or what not. God has decided that His Word should be taught, and that claim is His Law; the contention is whether the Papists or their opponents preach the Word of God or what is contrary to the Word of God, and which of the laws of God are in harmony with it and which are not. Therefore, that a murderer should be put to death is according to law; that remains and there is no question about that; further, if any-

---

[2] In D. S. there is a new paragraph here.

one has committed murder he is brought before the law, his defense is heard and inquiry is made as to whether he has acted against the law or not; and should he who preaches the true Word of God and offers to prove it have no trial? and that [trial] should be prevented by the most holy and most spiritual leaders? who, since they claim to be Christians, should be obligated to correct and instruct, with all gentleness, everyone who is in error; is this not an erroneous and insolent madness, which even the Turks would find disgusting?[3]

7

In addition, everyone knows very well what happened at the Council of Constance. All the princes and estates of the Empire, which the papist crowd calls secular, had been persuaded that it was not up to them to sit in judgment concerning matters of faith, and therefore this matter was relegated to the tonsured and cowl-clad prelates. If, then, they had recognized anything which, according to the Scriptures would have undermined their magnificent, lazy, cowardly, obstinate lives, it would have been against all the order of nature, which is always inclined to love itself more than others and to prefer the temporal to the eternal. The devout Emperor Siegmund would have liked very much to undertake the reformation of the spiritual estate and tried to do it with great zeal, but he was overruled by the so-called spiritual leaders, just as it still happens today, when they assemble together, that the papists have three votes when devout, secular princes, who offer their lives, honor and worldly goods for the sake of the Empire, do not even have one [vote]; and it seems that all things must take precedence over such a salutary reformation. For it is quite obvious that from heel to head there is nothing healthy nor whole in the entire so-called spiritual estate. And therefore it is in no way irresponsible if, quite apart from the decisions of the Council of Constance, the Word of God should be the sole guide of all teaching and preaching; and everyone who offers to prove that his preaching and teaching are the Word of God should be heard; espe-

---

[3] D. S. says, "Which would be too much for the Turks."

cially since it is not considered irresponsible in matters of far less importance, to examine what is according to or contrary to the Law, and that without any regard for the decisions of the old Fathers.

8

The Holy Scriptures are as clear as day, so that it is not difficult to realize when the so-called spiritual crowd teach and do anything contrary to the Scriptures; this is also recognized by the authorities as long as there is freedom to preach the Word of God, so that indeed no one who is well informed and no one who has not rejected the truth beforehand, would consider it useless or unnecessary in regard to matters of our faith and Christian life except those who now revel in discord and do not allow a trial, defense and cross-examination and acquittal. Yes, no one who loves Christ should reject these, much less condemn anyone without a trial. But to be sure, whoever thinks a little about these matters will soon see that the so-called spiritual leaders had no objection to anything which concerned their own prerogatives. They know that if they were to appear before the common[4] court,[5] and should their actions be held up against divine Scriptures, yes, even up to common decency, they wouldn't have a chance. Therefore, since the last *Reichstag* held in Augsburg, all their work and care have been concerned solely with this, that no one should receive a fair trial but everyone who did not agree with them should be condemned without justification and without trial.[6] Your Highness will no doubt recognize that this is not only anti-Christian but even unnatural; just as you have recognized and been concerned for a long time that those who call themselves spiritual have attempted with all their power to swing things their way; and therefore your soul will never agree to their counsels.

---

[4] "regular"
[5] *Gemeinehrbarkeit*
[6] In D. S. a new paragraph begins here.

9

Nor will you be moved by their ceaseless lies [claiming] that we want to abolish all authority, and that, should a reformation be achieved with them, we would attack all authorities and dissolve all obedience. For if the Word of God is preached, it will be taught that every single soul should be subject to and obey the powers and all authorities as it is stated in Romans 13:1, Titus 3:1, and 1 Peter 2:13. For surely anyone who learns to know God correctly will not countenance opposition to His government who establishes all powers and authorities. But they, the so-called spiritual leaders, if they really desire to be spiritual and apostolic, should, like Christ our Lord, serve and not rule; just as He did not allow anyone to serve Him but served us and gave His soul for the salvation of many and said to His disciples: "The worldly princes rule, and those who are in power use force; but it should not be like that amongst you, but if anyone among you wants to be considered powerful he should be your servant, and he who desires to be the greatest should be your servant" (Matt. 20:25–27). Now, however, they neglect the divine service of the divine Word and oppose with force all those who have been established by God as authorities and officials, yes, as Peter prophesied of them, "They walk according to the flesh in the lust of their impurity, despise the authorities, are impudent, think highly of themselves and do not tremble when they insult their majesties" (2 Peter 2:10). Therefore they are the ones who dissolve godly government and obedience, and destroy all authorities according to their own will, contrary to the Word of God, which teaches everyone, the circumcised and uncircumcised, that they should be subject to princes and those in power, and should obey the authorities.

10

At the present time and everywhere in Strasbourg, for the sake of peaceful cohabitation and Christian unity, our honorable Council, my gracious lords, have ordered the so-called spiritual leaders to act in civic unity and duty like other citizens, noble and common, yet there are many among them who claim that this is contrary to their oath and honor, just as if their oath and honor constrained them from being obedient to those amongst whom they live, yes, from whom they receive their sustenance and some of whom, according to descent, are their relatives; neither to be faithful nor kind, nor to be obedient to those commands and restrictions which serve and are necessary to honesty, respectability, decency, and modesty. For civic duty and solidarity, which have been entrusted to them, demand nothing more. As much as they insist upon their liberties, granted to them by kings and emperors, it is well known that these were granted only to the spiritual holy fathers, in order that they should be freer in the service of the divine Word, and in no way to such a loose[7] crowd which would be in greater need of an authority, and that a very strict one, than any other people on earth, as is quite obvious to those who have eyes to see. Look at their letters of release,[8] yes, all their ancient concessions, and you will find that similar ones have been made to many other people who are very much like our so-called spiritual crowd, in the same way in which Abraham was like the Pharisees who crucified Jesus.[9] But as has been indicated above, they justify in many ways that it is not proper to grant a public trial and defense in matters of faith, when all the while the real reason is that they fear such a public trial, since they know that basically their justifications are questionable and useless; and so in this matter they try to justify their position with this and that, and by doing so they really relinquish all divine and proper obedience, but the one true reason is that their lives are of such a kind that they are unable to accept any Christian authority which has been "established by God for the punishment of the evildoers and the reward of the good" (1 Peter 2:14), and this is why Paul also says in Romans 13:3: "the rulers should be feared not on account of good works but evil." And so we find that those so-called spiritual leaders are the very ones who despise and reject all divine authority, and this is because they cannot endure such an account of their unjust way of living, but attribute this falsely to the preachers of the Divine Word, who nevertheless teach and preach not only that they should be subject to

---

[7] D. S. says "cowardly"
[8] *Freiheitsbriefe*
[9] In D. S. a new paragraph begins here.

every properly instituted authority, but that they (who should not rule in a worldly way if they want to be in the line of the apostles, and since God has it so ordered that they are worldly lords) should be obeyed by all who are under their authority as long as they order nothing which is contrary to God and concerns the soul; yes, they should teach out of the Word of God only those matters which are temporal, such as body, honor and material things, nor should they employ force. But since their first concern is to deceive and mislead the poor, simple lay people, and since they with their deeds which they carry on shamelessly have for some time now been an abomination to all common decency, and no one who loves decency and modesty will want to have anything to do with them, they only prove that they have not been born of God but of the devil, for John says: "he who sins is of the devil," so it follows inevitably, yes, it can't be anything else but that all their fencing and protesting are nothing but lies. The devil is a liar and the father of lies (John 8:44); could he teach his sons anything other than that?

11

And they are extremely zealous in these matters here and everywhere. They have invented, stated and written so many awkward and unfounded lies concerning me, who am a poor and humble, unprepossessing servant of the Word, that it is almost unbelievable. They claim that I led a disorderly life in those days when I lived at the court of Your Excellency; they claim that surely I must have run away in great disgrace from Your Excellency's court, and yet I was graciously dismissed with gifts and presents; they claim that my wife deserted me; that I have circumcised children; that I have done this and done that. And they even dare to say to some princes that some of my co-workers in the Word had preached that our dear Lady, the Mother of Christ, is a female dog; and someone else claimed about another one of us that he had preached that if a man were separated from his wife for some time she should take the next best one who caught her fancy; we, however, have preached very clearly concerning our position in regard to marriage according to the Law of God, that if it were to be observed carefully, some of their so-called spiritual leaders would have had to leave the country long ago; for it is known concerning some of these highly learned and spiritual leaders that if someone has divorced his wife in their ecclesiastical courts, they turn around and take her into their homes.

12

And therefore, Gracious Lord, since there are some matters concerning the service of worship which have been changed and improved by my colleagues and preachers of the Gospel here in Strasbourg, in harmony with the true, eternal Word of God, and concerning which our opponents have lied abominably to princes and lords far and wide, just as they treated us prior to this, I have desired to write Your Highness very briefly concerning these things, with proofs from the divine Scriptures, which are our only source and authority, so that you, informed of the truth, would pay no attention to the stupid fairy tales, even though distinguished bishops and prelates should tell them, for in such matters they are much too gullible, and it must be affirmed and reaffirmed that these tales have been invented too readily. I have had the desire, as far as I have been able, to inform Your Highness that I am always ready and willing to do these things to serve and please you, for I retain and will always retain with indelible remembrance all the gracious favors which you have lavished on me, your unworthy servant.

13

And I address to you now my loyal, humble and diligent request that you graciously accept this my writing, written with deep Christian conviction, and that no one should turn you away from the eternal, true saving Word of God; as a distinguished Prince of the Empire you have not been tempted to listen to the rumors and complaints of the anointed ones, since you have learned to distinguish them by their fruits, both in the high and low estates, and you have condemned no one without a proper trial nor paid any regard to the station of the person. Christ says: "Who is highly exalted among men, is an abomination before God" (Luke 16:15). He has chosen for the proclamation of His Word from the beginning of time, the rejected and the lowly. Read 1 Corinthians 1:18–29 and 2:1–16. But we are so certain of our convictions, that we are willing to die if anyone should prove that our preaching and the actions which follow it are not in the closest harmony with the true Word of God written in His Holy Scriptures; and it is our greatest grievance that up to now our opponents have constantly hindered us everywhere, so that we have been unable to give to the whole world the reason and the justification[10] for our teaching and actions in the way in which we would best be able to do it. We seek the light and do not fear the light as do our opponents. The Almighty grant Your Highness, through Christ our Lord, to understand His Word rightly, to stand firm and remain in it, for the sake of your own welfare and salvation as well as that of your subjects. Amen.

Given at Strasbourg, the 26th of December, 1524.

Your Highness's most obedient servant,
Martin Butzer

---

[10] *Grund und Ursach*

Dear Christian Reader: So that no one may take offense, I will try my very best, not only to give the meaning of the Holy Scriptures, but even to quote them word for word. For this reason no one should be dismayed if he should read any words here other than the common usage. He should examine the Scriptures and he will discover that such words were inspired by the Holy Spirit, not invented by me.

I
Concerning the Innovations in the Lord's Supper

1. The Lord's Supper, as it is commonly called by the Holy Spirit through the mouth of Paul, has been called the Mass for a long time by the subjects of the Roman Catholic Church, and it has been explained to all and sundry that the priest, when he conducts the Mass, sacrifices the body and blood of Christ for the living and the dead; and no useful and salutary good work was taken into account. And in order to signify this sacrifice it has been the custom to elevate the bread and the chalice of the Lord, and for this reason it was not held in high regard, even though no one partook of the Lord's Supper; in addition, it was customary to use such vestments as were used by the officiants of the Jews and the pagans, in Latin they were called *sacerdotes*, so that the Mass, in every respect, was held to be and interpreted to be a sacrifice.

2. We, however, taught by the grace of God through His Holy Word (to Him be praise eternal) know that it is the most abominable, most poisonous and most harmful insult and slander of Jesus Christ our Lord and Savior, to believe and to say that the priest in the Mass offers Him as a sacrifice. Therefore, since light has nothing in common with darkness, and Christ has no communion with Belial, and the believer has no fellowship with the unbeliever (1 Cor. 6:15), in our churches we have completely done away with and abolished everything which has no basis in the Scriptures and which has been added to the Lord's Supper without any justification in the Scriptures and therefore has been an insult and a slander of Christ and of the divine mercies, so that we do not any longer use the name Mass, but the

Lord's Supper, which we celebrate as a remembrance of the death of Christ, and in no way consider a sacrifice of His body and blood; and we no longer elevate the bread and the chalice; and we no longer [celebrate the Lord's Supper] unless there are some present who partake of the bread and the cup of the Lord. In addition the priest and servant of the congregation does not wear a special vestment, only what we call the choir gown, and none of the sacrificial vestments such as alb, stole, chasuble, etc., nor do we use any special kind of gestures, which have been invented by men without any justification in the Word of God.

3. Since it is not good enough to do that which in itself is right and proper, but that which is the duty of a Christian, to see to it as far as possible that his actions as one of the elect be superior (to the lost ones that which is good has the smell of death), for true Christian love demands that we should ever be prepared to die for the good of our neighbor as the Lord did for us, and I need say no more to the effect that in other things we should strive to be their example. Paul, in Romans 14:19, encourages us to do just that. It is our duty, he says, that everyone among us should try to please his neighbor for his good, for his edification. For even Christ did not please Himself but, as it is written: "the insults of those who insult (you) have covered me." He further writes to the Corinthians in the same vein: "Whether you eat or drink or whatever you do: do not be an offense both to the Greeks and the Jews and the community of God, in the same way in which I, too, please everyone in all things and do not seek that which is profitable for me but for many, so that they be saved. Be my disciples, just as I am Christ's" (1 Cor. 10:31–11:1).

4. For this reason it has been our desire, as far as possible, where we have made changes and improvements in this and that by reference to the Word of God, to please and improve every man, so that, just as in itself it is correct and divine, and just as it is held and accepted by everyone to the glory of God, whose Word we have followed carefully in these things so that it may serve for the edification and growth of those who have given themselves to

Christ, they too desire to follow only the voice of their Shepherd and the teaching of the only Lord and Teacher sent to us by God, and to give secondary importance to those things invented by men, which relate to faith and worship. In addition it is our responsibility to watch and work with the utmost diligence, so that our treasure, the Holy Gospel and the eternal Word, yes, even our office, should not be slandered (Rom. 14:16 and 2 Cor. 6:3), so that all our actions should not only be pleasant and edifying to men of good will but, as far as it is possible to us, be beyond the reproach of the malevolent.

5. We do not know how to achieve both of these in a better and quicker way than by demonstrating to all through the Scriptures and God's Word, which we ourselves have first of all obeyed and followed in our actions: so that if the elect of God perceive this, how they can recognize and serve God the Lord as supreme, then they will also find delight in it, since then they obey His promise and commandment. With David the whole company of the faithful sings: "The laws of God are righteous altogether. They are more precious than gold and much fine gold, sweeter also than honey and the honeycomb…. How sweet are your words in my mouth, more than honey is to my mouth. I understand what you have commanded and therefore I hate all the ways of falsehood" (Pss. 19:10–11; 119:103). Therefore, since the lambs will hear the desired and beloved voice of their shepherd, they will immediately recognize it and will follow it with great desire, they will have delight and joy, because it has been given to us to follow His voice. No human authority, teaching or custom will be held in greater regard, we are bought dearly, and we are no longer subject to other men (1 Cor. 7:23). With body, honor and worldly goods we desire to be subject to and obey all human ordinances and authorities, but the Spirit should be surrendered to God, and just as no man can understand the ways and will of God, even so no one is able to teach us how and whereby we are to be acceptable to Him except He alone. Therefore David says in Psalm 119:130, 133: "If Thy Word, O Lord, goes forth it will enlighten and bring knowledge to the simple minded . . . Direct my ways through Thy Word." For this reason God has

earnestly forbidden in the fifth book of Moses "to do what will please every man.... All that I command you, you should keep; so that you act accordingly. You shall neither add to it nor take away from it" (Deut. 12:8, 32).

6. For this reason we are sure and without any doubt: whoever is devout when he reads the clear and bright words of God on which and according to which we have acted, and in regard to our innovations or rather our restorations of that which is right, old and eternal, he will not only have no objection to them but will praise and glorify God, who has delivered us from the swarm of so many improper and harmful ordinances and customs, and brought us again on His way and to His command, placing himself and others under the Word of God, and will encourage and bring others to the sole, clear Word of God and all things which pertain to the worship of God.

7. As far as the malevolent are concerned, we know no better way to undermine their attempt to slander the Word of God and our office. For they will have no delight in it when we show them clearly that God, who is ever the highest authority, has ordained and commanded what we have accomplished in innovations, or better still, in reforms: what else should we do with them than what Christ said in Matthew 15:14, to ignore them, the blind leaders of the blind? It is impossible for us to show them any higher command and law than the command and law of God; and whoever does not allow us to hold to this, we will not hold him in high regard. "We must obey God more than man" (Acts 5:29). Especially since God's demands cannot please them, it would be bad for us it our actions were to please them and were beyond reproach [to them]. We can do nothing else than be willing to defend our position to everyone who asks for the reasons of the hope which is in us, and to do so with gentleness and fear, as Peter teaches. Whoever refuses to accept these things and completely disregards the Word of God, regards man's customs and ordinances higher than the command and will of God, and him we must commit to the judgment of God,[11] and

---

[11] D. S. footnote: "and even if such heretics and offenders insult us."

even when they call us heretics and offenders, this should concern us in no way, since the mob called even Jesus, the Head of the Household, Beelzebub.

8. Therefore I conclude that whoever does not disregard natural decency and fairness, will not condemn us without a hearing or before listening to our justification. When he then perceives that it is founded on the true Word of God and the expressed command of God, he will be unable to pursue [the argument] any further. But whoever cannot be convinced in such a way, as many stupid people cannot, and will in no way listen to our justification and will condemn our actions without knowledge of the facts: people like that we will neither esteem nor fear; for they neither esteem nor fear God, yes, they even act contrary to all natural decency. But to those whom God has neither rejected nor blinded, we will declare and present, out of divine Scriptures, the reasons for our actions, so that they will recognize us as their Christian brothers and fellow members, and will love and defend us against everyone. It is to serve and please them that we have written this document.

II
Concerning the Name of the Lord's Supper

9. Firstly, our brothers detest the name "Mass" and customarily call it the Lord's Supper,[12] which according to the Roman custom we have heretofore called the Mass. To be sure, we do not wish to quarrel with anyone over words. We are much more concerned to deal with the thing itself, for such quarreling about words brings along with it hatred, disputes and other things, and as a result Christian faith and love are destroyed (1 Tim. 6:4); we must also confess that it is more Christian and more accurate that we call that which Christ our Lord has instituted by the name given to it in the Scriptures, rather than use a word concerning which we are unable to de-

---

[12] *Nachtmal des Herrn*

termine its original meaning anywhere. Some believe that *Missa*, which we in German call Mass, is a Hebrew word from the root word *Mas,* which means an obligatory gift such as a tribute, and means a sacrifice, and so it is used in the fifth book of Moses (Deut. 16:1–17). And therefore, since it is the most abominable abomination to consider the Lord's Supper a sacrifice, we can do nothing else than utterly reject and condemn such a name. But since this name is not used by the Greek Fathers, who call the Lord's Supper *liturgian,* that is, an office or service, and since the old Latin authors such as Cyprian and Jerome and others do not use the word, it is very doubtful that such a name derives from Hebrew, since the Greek Fathers, the first students of Hebrew, and the old Latin Fathers surely would have used it.

10. No matter what its origin or by what name it is called, and since there is no certainty about its origin, one thing is sure: it is not in Holy Scriptures; and this alone is sufficient reason why Christians should reject and abolish it. And it seems to us that it is through the will of God that as a result of the false and misleading opinion, namely that in the Lord's Supper His body and blood are sacrificed by the priest, the world had been so blinded that it no longer knew what the Lord's Supper was or what its benefit was, and therefore it was given a name whose origin and meaning no one knew or understood. Since, then, there can be "no fellowship between light and darkness" (2 Cor. 6:14), we who are the children of light should completely reject not only the darkness and its works, but also the names it uses. David says in Psalm 16:4: "their drink offerings of blood I will not sacrifice, neither take up their names in my mouth." Consequently, we too, who have such a horror of presuming to sacrifice the body and blood of Christ again, also have a horror of using such names as sacrificer, sacrifice, work, which they customarily use.

11. We know that it is the Spirit of God alone which knows what is divine (1 Cor. 2:11), and therefore no one should call these things anything else. Therefore, since He calls it the Lord's Supper, we too should use no other name and should in no way attempt to teach the Holy Spirit and to apply

strange names to His activities, since it is impossible for us to know them and their origin except only by the spirit of error and untruth. If the name used and interpreted by the Mass-lovers had been good for anything, the Holy Scriptures would in no way have refrained from using it, for Scripture teaches more than sufficiently that which is useful and good. And therefore we teach [people] to call it, as does the Spirit of God, the Lord's Supper, and not the Mass, so that our actions and our words may be in harmony with the Holy Scriptures. However, we admonish that no one should start a quarrel over the name or that anyone should condemn the others as long as, along with the name, they do not accept also the error, that we give and sacrifice anything to God. This is our teaching and the reason why we have abolished and discarded the name Mass; so that everyone should use the term the Supper of the Lord,[13] as 1 Corinthians 11:20 calls it.

III

That the Lord's Supper Should Be Held as a Memorial of the Death of Our Lord and in no Way as a Sacrifice

12. It is a most pernicious and most abominable error to believe that in the Lord's Supper the body and blood of Christ are sacrificed, as has been cited in so many publications, and furthermore, it is so preached without ceasing wherever the Word of God is known, and thus it is unnecessary to quote many writings. The words of Christ are clear. When He took the bread, gave thanks and broke it, He said, "Take, eat, this is my body which is broken for you. Do this in remembrance of me." After the same manner also the cup after the supper and said, "This cup is a New Testament in my blood. Do this as oft as you drink it, in remembrance of me" (1 Cor. 11:23–25). These are the words of the Lord as Paul had received them from the Lord, by which everyone can see that the Lord commands only two things, namely, for one, to eat the bread and to drink the cup; the other, to do this in remembrance of Him; such remembrance, as long as it is done sincerely,

---

[13] *Nachtmahl des Herrn*

brings along with it, by itself, the proclamation of the death of Christ, for who could contemplate and believe this to be his eternal salvation without immediately desiring earnestly to sing and speak about it to everyone? Therefore, immediately following the above words of the Lord, Paul says: "For as oft as you eat of this bread and drink of this cup, you proclaim the Lord's death until He come" (1 Cor. 11:26). And since, then, we do not want to add to or take away from the words of the Lord, and just as in these matters we know nothing by ourselves except what He has revealed to us, it is only fitting that we adhere strictly to the command of the Lord, namely, that when we observe the Lord's Supper we receive the bread and the cup of the Lord and in so doing remember His death and proclaim it, and do not presume to sacrifice anything which the Lord has not mentioned with a single word.

13. Luke, too, in the Acts of the Apostles 2:42, where he describes how the faithful acted and where he speaks about the Lord's Supper—as it was observed everywhere, and transmitted in words—writes: "They remained steadfastly in the Apostles' teaching, in the fellowship, and in the breaking of the bread and in prayer." Notice, then, he calls it quite simply, "the breaking of the bread," and does not say: to sacrifice in the bread, or something similar. Let him who does not want to be quarrelsome note, also, that the breaking of the bread is mentioned in connection with the Apostles' teaching, the communion, and bread, and let him admit that the Lord's Supper is meant; for to speak of the eating of common food in connection with such high spiritual things would be ridiculous and completely contrary to the intention of the apostles. And just because he speaks about breaking of the bread alone, this does not mean that the communion of the cup is excluded; but on the contrary that it is taken for granted, for it should be accepted fully that in such breaking of the bread they were completely in harmony with the institution of Christ and therefore in no way omitted the communion of the cup.

14. However this may be, it cannot be denied that Paul was speaking about the Lord's Supper when he says in 1 Corinthians 10:16: "the cup of blessing which we bless, is it not the communion of the blood of Christ? The bread which we break, is it not the communion of the body of Christ?" He does not say: the cup which we sacrifice, but the cup which we bless, that is to say, the cup over which we praise and glorify God; he does not say: the bread which we sacrifice, but: the bread which we break, that is to say, divide to eat, according to the custom of the country to break bread in order to eat it.

15. Now then, since it is impossible for us to know anything of the institution of Christ other than what is revealed by His Spirit in the Scriptures, it should be quite sufficient for us to reject the meaning of a sacrifice as an undoubted invention of the devil and to reject utterly and completely that Christ our Lord ever taught a single word about sacrificing, but commanded only to take it, and in doing so, to remember Him and thus to follow the example of David, when he says: "I love Thy commandments more than gold and much fine gold. Therefore I follow strictly that which you have commanded. I hate every false path" (Ps.119:127–128), and if all this is not sufficient: He who is not convinced by what we have said, let him read the Scriptures and he will find that all Scriptures point to the one and only sacrifice of Christ, when He sacrificed His body on the cross, through which enough is done for the elect, and not a single word that such a body should be sacrificed a thousand times daily by the priests. But Scripture does teach everywhere that we should daily sacrifice our own bodies, a broken spirit and a contrite heart, to the praise of God.

16. In Hebrews 9:24–28 we read: "Christ did not enter into the Holy Place made with hands, which is a reflection of the true (eternal) one, but into Heaven itself to appear before the face of God. Nor yet that He should sacrifice Himself many times just as the High Priest enters every year into the Holy Place with the blood of strangers, otherwise He would have had to suffer often from the beginning of the world, but at the end of the world He

will appear once to take away the sins through His own sacrifice, and just as it is appointed for man to die once and after that the Judgment, so, too, Christ has been sacrificed once to take away the sins of many, but hereafter He will appear without sin to those who wait for Him for salvation."

17. What could be clearer than this which is said against the foolish sacrifice of the Mass? Where are the Mass-lovers, the poor, inflated fools[14] who presume to sacrifice Christ daily? Listen, Christ does not offer Himself many times, otherwise He would have to suffer many times. From this it follows that, if you want to sacrifice Him daily, He will also have to suffer daily, and you will have to crucify Him daily, and this is exactly what so many of you do daily, you poor Christ-murderers. And after this you hear too that at the end of the world He will appear once and remove the sins through His own sacrifice. Why do you say, then, that He should appear daily in your bloody, murdering hands, many thousands of times again as a sacrifice? On the contrary, the Apostle says that He had appeared through His own sacrifice; how dare you then say that He is your sacrifice? Your own cowardly, self-willed, detrimental body, that should be your sacrifice, you sacrificers to Baal!

18. Finally, you hear that He appeared in order to remove sin. And since He, by His own sacrifice, has removed the sins of many, namely of all the elect, how dare you to trouble so many poor souls with so many despairing, blasphemous Masses? Can't you understand, you sowers of sins who in no way can take away sins, that just as man must die once and after that the Judgment, even so Christ has been sacrificed once to take away the sins of many? What in the world do you think you accomplish with your sacrifices? Christ Himself has taken away the sins with His sacrifice offered once-for-all. Why then don't you realize that with your sacrifices you do nothing more than sow and plant sins and cover the world with unbelief and all sorts of vices? And that is exactly what you have done!

---

14 *Bauchfolk*

19. You have driven the people away from their faith in the Christ sacrificed once-for-all, and have turned them to your sacrifices, have appointed yourselves as the only legitimate, consecrated sacrificers and have robbed the whole world of their property; and so that it would never again be theirs, who have earned it with the sweat of their brow, you have rejected the estate of matrimony; and you live in a state of impurity unheard of in the rest of the world. Furthermore, you condemn and persecute the Word of God, so that by such doings you hide your blasphemous temptations, deception and impure living. And you use your sacrifice of the Mass to support and defend this. Consequently there is no doubt about it that you, with your sacrifice of the Mass, have covered the world with sins. Even if there were no such [Mass], because you live in such shameless knavery, common decency would have long ago refused to put up with you, and I will say nothing [about the fact] that you have been permitted to acquire such wealth and power by means of which you have opposed everything which is godly and honorable.

20. Therefore, he who has a heart and a soul and does not despair of his salvation and all the good gifts of God, would do better to flee from this most blasphemous and most destructive error, in the same way in which he would flee hell and the most dangerous poison through which all faith and piety are killed. But take comfort in the holy, apostolic words: "Once-for-all Christ has sacrificed Himself for sin, and that is eternally valid…with it He has perfected the holy ones in all eternity" (Heb. 10:12, 14), that is, the elect whom God has chosen from the world.

21. And if someone should say: the Epistle to the Hebrews was not considered by the Fathers to be equal in value to the accepted writings, such as the four Gospels and the other epistles of Paul, just as Eusebius and Origen claim, I say that these two and Clement of Alexandria, who lived close to the time of the Apostles, bear witness that the Latin Fathers, who were never well instructed in divine things, omitted this epistle from the other Pauline epistles. And Eusebius mentions another writer, Gaius, who lists only

thirteen epistles of Paul; but the ancient worthies from the time of the Apostles have always accepted it without question as an epistle of Paul. But all agree unanimously that it was Paul who first wrote it in the Hebrew language and afterwards it was translated into Greek, some claim by Luke, the evangelist, and others by Clement (Eusebius, 3:3; 6:11, 12).

22. Be all this as it may, what the Epistle to the Hebrews says is nothing else than what is contained in all the rest of the Holy Scriptures, namely that through the once-for-all death of Christ, when He sacrificed Himself once for all of us, all the elect are cleansed and saved. "All we like sheep have gone astray, everyone has strayed away from his way, and the Lord has laid on Him all our unrighteousness. He went Himself, willingly, and did not open His mouth; He will be led to His sacrificial death like a sheep…. Since He gave His soul for sin, He will see a long-lasting seed, and the pleasure of the Lord will succeed in His hand. Since His soul has had travail, He will see (His delight) and will be satisfied; through His insight He will justify many of my servants and will bear their unrighteousness" (Isa. 53:6–7, 10–11).

23. In these words we see very clearly that through His death, sacrificed like a lamb, Christ has taken away the sins of the elect. But this happened only once, and no Scripture passage says that He should be sacrificed again and again; but the prophet says that the favor of God lies in His hand, that is, through His power and spirit, He would succeed and be happy ever after, because He once offered His soul for sins; and in this knowledge which He grants to the elect servants of God, through which they know and believe that He died once-for-all for them, through this they are justified. This means nothing other than this: if He grants us to remember His death and to believe that He suffered death for us, through which we have been accepted as the children of God, then we shall be righteous before God and shall be saved, and in no wise through a repeated sacrifice. Of this there is not a single word in all Scripture, so that, as was mentioned above, if there is no mention anywhere, this should be enough to [make us] flee the abom-

ination of the repeated sacrifice as the worst deception of the devil. Since the Scriptures contain all that is good, it follows that anything which is added certainly comes from the devil and is the rankest poison for faith. And this is quite evident from the fruits of this abomination, which have been mentioned briefly above, namely, that through it the shorn riffraff,[15] opposing faith and all decency, have become great, numerous and powerful.

24. Therefore, it is certain and is maintained through the true Word of God, that in the Lord's Supper we should think with faith and thanksgiving of His death and His sacrifice, that He sacrificed Himself to the Father once and for all on the cross for the sins of all the elect. This should be remembered with faith and thanksgiving; this should be the content of our preaching and our praise of God, and no one should presume to offer anything else, as is done by the children of damnation. To counter this the Mass-lovers can say nothing that is valid. For even though they produce many people, yes, present their own fabrications, how can that prevail against the Word of God, which alone is the foundation of our teaching and actions? Man is vain and a liar; God alone is true and just.

25. All Scripture from these latter days, after the departure of the Apostles, has prophesied that abominable errors will creep in, so that "even the elect, where this could be done, would be led into error" (Matt. 24:24). And it is easy to see that for this rabble no effort is too great, although all their actions are contrary to the actions of Christ, just as water is opposed to fire, and they even put themselves in the seat of Christ and appropriate all His power and His honor; therefore everyone should be very suspicious about what they under take or defend. They are evil, lazy, poisonous trees; how can they bear any good fruit?

26. It is true that some of the devout, holy fathers accepted the same errors, and it is no wonder that in these difficult days fraud and iniquity predomi-

---

[15] *i. e.*, the priests (*das beschoren gesind*).

nate, just as the Lord Himself so dreadfully prophesied in Matthew 24:4–12. The saints are constantly surrounded by sins and error, so that the praise should be given to the mercy of God alone. James, the great apostle, and also the Christians in Jerusalem, were in such dreadful error after they had received the Spirit of God and after they had preached for many years, since they believed that those Jews who accepted Jesus Christ were also required to observe the law of Moses as is stated in Acts 15:5 and in 11:2–3, the Christians quarreled with Peter regarding circumcision because he had preached Christ to the Gentiles, even though Christ had commanded them to go into the whole world to preach the Gospel.

27. It is true that the Mass-lovers will have difficulty in finding many saints who believed that one sacrifices anything in the Lord's Supper, and they wouldn't find anyone at all who would not reject and condemn their godless, lumpy Masses[16] which they sing and read only to sustain their bellies and their cowardly lives. And although [both] are found often in the Fathers, the little word *sacrificium*, sacrifice, and *sacrificare vel offerre*, that is, to sacrifice, refers commonly to this, that in it the once-for-all sacrifice of Christ is remembered, which, if it is accepted in faith, will bring the fruit of the sacrifice of Christ, namely forgiveness of sins and all mercies. For truly: the body of Christ is given for us, and we will be partakers of Him and receive its benefit, when in true faith we recognize and meditate upon it that Christ has sacrificed His body and blood for our sins once on the cross. On Christmas Day we sing, "Christ is born today," and think only of His birth. Therefore it should not be such a surprise to those who read the Fathers, when they read that the Fathers write that Christ is sacrificed in the Lord's Supper, especially since the Lord's Supper is nothing other than a memorial of such a sacrifice through which, if it is accepted in true faith, the benefits of the sacrifice are obtained.

---

[16] *batzen messen* (half-baked)

28. Furthermore, it can be observed that the old Latin Fathers, when they found no terms in their language to describe Christian matters, used names which were meaningful to the pagans whenever these things corresponded to Christian matters. Therefore they gave names to the description of the faith and acceptance of baptism which were in use when the Romans accepted nobility,[17] yes, they even adopted mannerisms and gestures and Christianized them. In the same way, since there were similarities between pagan sacrifices and the Lord's Supper, they called it *sacrificium,* that is, a sacrifice, for just as the pagans honored their gods in their sacrifices, ate together and refreshed their friendship with joy, even so when the Lord's Supper is observed correctly, it is done with praise and thanksgiving, and in the same way with the holy food and drink when Christians renew their spiritual and eternal covenant and testament in the Lord; and so they could have said: the pagans have their *sacrificia* and sacrifices, when they assemble together to honor their gods; our *sacrificia* is the Lord's Supper, in which we do not sacrifice anything to God except our own selves, but we recall at that time the sacrifice which was offered once-for-all for us and has eternal validity. In doing so we proclaim the Lord's death, give Him praise and glory *(Lob und Preis)* and encourage one another in love and good deeds, since we are one bread and one body in Christ.

29. He who does not want to get involved in useless arguments and reads the Fathers such as Tertullian, Cyprian and others with a sincere heart, will have to admit that this is true. He who wants to quarrel, however, to him we must say that his authorities are people, who are as nothing in comparison with the Word of God. Whatever they say is as nothing, if it is contrary to the Word of God.

30. When some, however, quote the prophet Malachi 1:11, namely, that if the name of the Lord be exalted among the pagans, a pure sacrifice should be offered in all places; by so doing they speak concerning the sacrifice of

---

[17] *Ritterschaft*

the body, which produces faith and knowledge of the divine Name in all places and all people; the evidence for this is not only the words of the prophet himself when he prophesies concerning the rejection of the Jewish people and the acceptance of the heathen, but also in many other writings, many of which are quoted by Tertullian in *Libro primo adversus Judaeos*.

31. By now it should be quite clear and abundantly proved and supported by the true Word of God, and no man or angel can prove otherwise, that the meaning and teaching that in the Lord's Supper Christ again sacrifices His body and His blood is a blasphemous and most harmful invention of the devil and of the true anti-Christ, in order to kill and to destroy to the utmost the faith and good works by means of which the most harmful rabble are maintained and strengthened for the destruction of all decency and the persecution of the children of God. Therefore, after we have been graciously enlightened by this knowledge from God, it has been impossible for us to tolerate such an abomination, and we cannot help but preach against it, and with the strong Word of God, which is impartial, having no regard for persons, tear it out of the hearts of the listeners, for one should listen to and fear only the Word of God. We have no doubt that those who have not been rejected by God will warmly approve of us, and particularly when they hear our justification for bringing about, not innovations, but a necessary and salutary reformation and restoration of the old and the eternal, and will join us in giving praise and thanks to God the Father for such mercy and knowledge, and will join us in directing and encouraging all others to do the same. May the Lord grant this. Amen.

IV
Reason for Abolishing the Elevation

32. Having been enlightened with certainty and sufficiency by the true Word of God, to which all things are subordinated, that it is the worst kind of abomination to believe that the body and blood of Christ are sacrificed in the Lord's Supper, we cannot do anything other than be completely dis-

gusted with everything which serves and strengthens such abomination and error. Among these not the least is the elevation of the bread and the cup of Christ, for with the elevation it is as much as indicated and proclaimed that the priest does sacrifice the body and the blood of Christ to God the Father, and this is proved by the words which are customarily used by the priests in the canon both before and after the elevation.

33. There are some who believe that this elevation is derived from the Law of Moses, in which the commandment was given to lift up some portion of the sacrificial oblation and the fat in the sin offering called *truma*; the reference for this is Leviticus 2:9 and 4:8. It is my opinion, however, that the Romans, in all their ceremonies, of which they have invented a countless number, have imitated and followed pagan practices more than those commanded to the Jews by God, just as they have never held Holy Scriptures in high regard. And from these idolatrous practices they have further adopted the burning of candles, the light Mass, many processions, all sorts of festivals, the tonsure of the priests, strange vestments, ostentatious funerals and countless other things, and they did not only find these in the Law of Moses, but even adopted them contrary to it. These dunces have presumed to obscure and to reverse the divine commands for all mankind and for this reason it is very seldom that they justify their actions by the Scriptures, but do it contrary to the clear prohibition of God in the Deuteronomy 12:1–4; 8; 29–32; everything which they did previously in front of their gods and idols they later did in the worship of God, and they made sure at all times that it was profitable for them. So then, although I do not want to quarrel with anyone about this, I have no doubt that this is what happened with the elevation.

34. And since nothing should be changed for salvation and reform unless it is done with faith, so that one may know and realize that it is thus proper and pleasing to God, before abolishing the elevation and other things like it which have been instituted without any justification in the Word of God and are external things, we have preached the Word of God and the Scrip-

tures diligently, for it is only in this way that any knowledge and insight come. In the meantime we have continued to elevate the bread and the cup and have continued to use vestments and some other Papist customs, but have always said and witnessed that we would continue to retain and use these customs for the sake of the weaker brethren until they, too, would be more perfectly instructed through the Word, to the effect that it would be far better to omit and do away with these matters, and have continued with great diligence to exhort everyone, when we lifted up the bread and the cup of Christ, that they should remember how Christ was lifted up on the cross for us and was offered as a sacrifice to the Father once, and that they should in no way think that we wanted to sacrifice the body and the blood of Christ over again through such an elevation.

35. Such patient waiting has been completely misunderstood by some, who for this reason have called us "double papists" (two-faced), even though it seems to us that they were able to offer nothing better prior to this waiting. We know that through the death of Christ we have been set free and are unencumbered by such poor concepts of the world, that is, requirements in regard to external matters, as Paul constantly reassures the Galatians 4:3, 9 and also the Colossians 2:20, and consequently to the pure all things are pure, as he writes to Titus 1:15, and therefore we should and must serve our neighbor freely in all things; others allow such practices and we admit that it might be good for them. Paul would never of his own accord have circumcised Timothy, for he knew that we were free from all such external requirements and that they were not necessary for salvation; and he preached this kind of freedom for he knew that one should put these things into practice and should be a good example to the weaker brethren; but since such freedom was unknown to the Jews at Lystra and Lyconium, he circumcised Timothy for the sake of those Jews; this he did, without any doubt, in order to retain their good will until such time as he could instruct and enlighten them in all things through the Word, and by doing so would win them over, just as he writes about himself "I have become all things to all men in order to save some" (1 Cor. 9:22). And for the same reason he made a vow and cut

his hair at Cenchrea (Acts 18:18), and submitted to the Jewish purification (Acts 21:26).

36. And if our opponents say that in these matters Paul had given in to some extent to the weaker brethren, but that these had been matters which God had previously commanded, and that for this reason the Jews had every right to cling to them; but those matters which we claim to tolerate for the sake of the weaker brethren had been invented and proclaimed by the anti-Christ to whom no one owed any allegiance for any reason at all. Answer: this kind of talk even the weaker brethren would recognize as finding its origin in the anti-Christ. However, since they know as little about these things as those Jews, to the effect that their external regulations should be abolished, and believe no less that it is against God if such ceremonies were done away with, just as those (believe) who did not keep their external commands, I myself do not see why we, like Paul with his (weaker brethren), may not and should not give in just as much to our weaker brethren who cling to human ordinances which they believe find their origin in the Spirit of God.

37. Furthermore, it is quite clear that after the beginning of the Kingdom of Christ, that is to say, after the public preaching of the Gospel, it was just as superstitious to consider the human statutes of Moses necessary as if these had been revealed through a human being. Therefore Paul in Colossians 2:8–23 gives as the command and teaching of men, matters such as circumcision, food laws and such other external practices commanded in the Law of Moses, for this reason that now, since we with Christ have died to them, they are no longer observed for the sake of God but only for the sake of other people, for in both, the freedom won for us through the blood of Christ would be denied and obscured; for one thing alone is needful, namely to hear and to accept the Gospel of Christ. Our weakness and theirs are one and the same thing, namely that they do not have a perfect understanding of Christ, for if they knew that it is He and He alone who does all things, they would consider all other things of equal value, and even if the Pope or

Moses had commanded them; for even at the time of Paul the commandments of Moses by themselves were as little the commandments of God as those which the Pope has given.

38. For this reason Christ, who in no way required them as necessary for salvation, is just as little denied as the demands of the Pope, even though the former found their origin in God and the latter in the anti-Christ; it is for this reason that Paul in Galatians 4:9 calls them beggarly requirements. As to their source, there is probably a greater difference between the ceremonies of Moses and those of the Pope, yet the weakness of faith is the same in both, for at the time of Paul the weak brethren held them to be necessary for salvation, which was not so; and in the same way today many good and kind people are opposed to Papist ordinances.

39. Paul himself knew very well that circumcision and other ceremonies of the Law were useless in themselves and were even harmful if too much reliance were placed on them, and that more time would be required for Christian freedom to be accepted, and yet he permitted the circumcision of Timothy, a disciple whose faith was held in highest regard, and he himself, who was farther advanced in his faith, still accepted some ceremonies for the time being so that he would not repel the weaker brethren until he could reveal Christ more perfectly to them: we too believe wholeheartedly that in regard to the observance of some ceremonies we should wait patiently for the sake of the weaker brethren and have the fullest justification to do so and feel that we have committed no sins; just the same, we are not looking for any kind of justification, however much we have tried to defend our actions. For even though we are not conscious of any wrongdoing, we are nevertheless not justified in this. It is very difficult in these matters to maintain a balance, and therefore we pray with David "Who can discern our sins? Cleanse me from all secret faults" (Ps. 19:13). We hope, however, that we have given no reason to chide us as double (two-faced) Papists. It is our greatest desire to advance only the glory of Christ. The only way in which we can do this is through the Word. In order to preach it acceptably,

we have tolerated a few ceremonies for the sake of the weaker brethren, even though they have been invented by the Papists with the worst kind of intention, and have been responsible for a great deal of detriment and harm to faith; nonetheless they are external matters and therefore in themselves they are harmless when they are not used in unbelief or to cause offense.

40. To eat food sacrificed to idols in the temples of idols was invented by the devil and was used for the destruction of all good things; and Paul confesses quite impartially that such things were prohibited with the greatest strictness in the Law of Moses, that it was allowed to the Christians, for the idol is nothing, and the sacrifice to or of idols was also nothing, as long as this was done with the intention of having no evil communion with idols, and that everyone should take care that by doing so he would not fall; but on the contrary the Apostle teaches that this should be done without offending the weaker brethren, that is, those who do not yet know such freedom, but in spite of this participate, against their conscience, and by doing so they sin when they participate with a bad conscience and without faith. From this it follows without doubt that if he had hoped that by eating sacrifices offered to idols in the temples of idols he would be in a better position to proclaim Christ to the pagans, no doubt he himself would have gone there, just as he did not forbid others to go there, as long as it would not be a cause for the weaker brethren to participate against their conscience and in doing so to sin, just as he permitted Timothy to be circumcised in order to open the way to preach freely to the Jews. Therefore, even though anti-Christ invented the elevation and used it to the destruction of godliness, because he thereby confirmed his blasphemous error concerning the sacrificing of the body and the blood of Christ, nonetheless we know that such an elevation is nothing in itself, just as the idols and their sacrifices were nothing in themselves, and that we Christians have all authority, as is so beautifully taught by Paul in 1 Corinthians 8:4–13 and 10:22–23. Surely, no one should condemn us if we have retained some ceremonies for a while for the sake of, or as an accommodation to the weaker brethren, in order to clear the way for the preaching of the Word of God.

41. And now I hear some say: How is it? Are you afraid that the Word of God in itself would be a hindrance? The Word of God is able to empower all Christians to act in all things according to the Word of God; when now you act and abolish what has been established without the Word, aren't you afraid that by doing so you will hinder the Word? Undoubtedly the lambs will know the voice of the shepherd. Answer: this argument could have been used against Paul when he had Timothy circumcised for the sake of the Jews, or again when he made a vow and later cut his hair at Cenchrea. Wouldn't it have been possible to say: How is it, dear Paul? You have no Word to allow a Christian, and such a famous brother, to be circumcised, when the Word directs everywhere that we should ignore these weak, beggarly ordinances; follow them, and don't pay any attention to what the Jews say, for the Lord knows His own (2 Timothy 2:19); it will be no hindrance to the Word if you act in accordance with the Word.

42. Paul, however, would have answered: My dear brethren, it is true that it would be no hindrance to the Word to act in accordance with the Word; we, however, are concerned to act in accordance with the Word "knowledge puffs up, but love edifies" (1 Cor. 8:1). It is quite true that no one should undertake anything which he has not first learned from the Word. Therefore, since these things concern only myself and my dear son Timothy, who understands Christian freedom, I was not at all eager to have him circumcised nor to cut my own hair; but the Word of God teaches me also that I should love my neighbor as Christ loved me and that I should be prepared out of love and service for Him either to do or not do all things, and what is more, I have the Word that the earth is the Lord's and all that is therein; therefore for us Christians all material things are subject to us and not we to them, "to the pure all things are pure" (Titus 1:15), and, therefore, I am perfectly free to circumcise, to make vows and to cut my hair.

43. Far be it from me to undertake such things, or that I should think that they in themselves are necessary for salvation, but since I have been made free from them through the death of Christ, I feel obliged to make use of

them whenever I hope that they may serve to edify. But I know all the while that the Lord knows His lambs and they, too, know His voice, and that He Himself must preach the Word to them, and that then He will reveal how I should act; further, since herein I should be His servant, and a true and wise servant whom He has set over His household, to give them food at the right time, then I must consider myself to be a co-worker, servant, a true and faithful slave and a steward of the divine mysteries; and just as my Master Christ would not crush the broken reed nor extinguish the glowing wick, but would graciously receive and carry the weak ones who are in the faith and would in love and service either do or not do what is in itself not against the law of God and what is neither against faith nor love; such as circumcision, cutting the hair and things like that.

44. It is no doubt true that my Master and Lord Christ could convert whom he pleases without my preaching and surely would not have need of my service nor of my actions nor my words. Therefore I do not act without the Word; the Word liberates me from external things and commands me to use them for the edification of the neighbor and therefore although I am not subject to anyone, yet I have made myself everyone's slave in order to win many of them: to the Jews I have become a Jew, to the weak a weakling, and all things to all men, so that I may win some and save them (1 Cor. 9:19–20, 22).

45. Who would condemn Paul for a reply like this? Well then, we also hope that if there is no mischief done, even though in some matters we have become popish with the Papists and have, for a time tolerated the elevation and some other practices which have been put to evil use by evil people but which in themselves are indifferent, and have suffered their use for a while, as has been stated, for the service and pleasure of those others, and have retained them until we were able to proclaim Christ to them better and would win them. In an attempt to win others one should deal carefully with the Scriptures, it is not written: faith comes from action, but with the preaching of the Word (Rom. 10:17). Josiah was king and had full authority, but he did

not abolish the abominations and idolatries until he first read the Book of the Covenant out aloud before the assembled people, and until he had reestablished the covenant with the Lord, and until all people had consented to the covenant. Read in the other book of the 2 Kings 23:1–25. If anyone desires to deal with the Word of God he should make sure as far as this is possible, with the help of God, that he has hearers. To be sure, God could draw all men to Himself. We however must serve Him in this; He must teach them all, we however must preach and be wise, so that we divide and distribute the word of truth properly, to the children as milk, to the mature as meat.

46. And what we read in Moses we certainly should understand and interpret as if Christ had said: "A new commandment I give unto you, just as I have loved you, that you should love one another…. In the little word: Love your neighbor as yourself, the whole Law is fulfilled" (John 13:34; Gal. 5:14). The Law of Moses commanded that they should tear down the altars of the pagans, upset their pillars, burn their idols with fire (Deut. 7:5). Paul also, when he entered Athens and saw that the city was very idolatrous, and even though his spirit within himself was angry, did not tear down a single altar, neither did he burn a single idol, but he preached to them and showed them that in all things they were much too superstitious. For one should take care to consider carefully the circumstances of all ordinances in order to differentiate between the temporal and the eternal. Those people were surrendered into the hands of the Israelites in order to be utterly destroyed; but the apostles were commanded to convert the pagans to Christ in order that, just as those used force, these should act through the Word. Wherever there is superstition, by whatever name it is called, be they Jews or pagans or Christians, (it does not really matter that we are called Christians but that we truly are Christians) we, too, must handle the Word of God in such a way that Christ is fully known, so that the abolition of human inventions should strengthen our trust in Christ, and should not frighten anyone away from the Word, excepting only the outcasts and vessels of the divine wrath, who never, ever may enter.

47. In these matters the right proportion is hardly ever kept, yet he who trusts in God, practices and obeys the Word of God with all sincerity, and is a careful shepherd of the flock of Christ, him the Lord will enlighten so that he too will not depart too far from the right proportion. For it is by the Spirit that those who are the children of God are led (Rom. 8:14), and He will teach them that they should always observe with their deeds what they teach in words. But first of all they will teach trust in the one and only Christ; and they will at once prove it in their deeds and put their trust in nothing else. Further, they will teach that in order to serve God one should undertake nothing which God Himself has not taught, and then they will also do it; in regard to all ceremonies they will not observe a single one in order to win the favor of God. But since they further teach that a Christian is the lord of the Sabbath and the lord of all external things, they will demonstrate this in their actions and will never be ensnared but prove by their actions that all things should be done out of love and service for the neighbor in order to please him in all good things; this must then also correspond with the actions, so that in matters which are external and do not in themselves cause our neighbor unbelief or scandal, it should not be difficult to observe them for a time, for the sake of the neighbor's pleasure and edification.

48. Would to God, however, that all those who accuse us of being too slow in these matters, such as the abolition of some ceremonies, and want to have all matters acted upon immediately, would conquer their old Adam first of all and give evidence that their own flesh has been crucified, and practice brotherly love in deed and be just as industrious to do good works; then there would be, God willing, more peace and unity, and His Word would not be blasphemed. O Lord, how difficult it is to come to the point where we dislike ourselves, but, like Christ, desire only to live in such a way as to please others! And this is our answer to those who maintain that we have waited too long with the abolition of the elevation and other Popish cere-

monies. I have stated the principles[18] of our faith in these matters, hoping all along that the faithful would be quite satisfied with our reasons. And I have done this in great detail for the reason that there are not a few who do not want to understand that love is the fulfilling of the Law (Rom. 13:10), and that all things are pure to the pure, an instead insist with firmness that the letter of the Law be observed when it concerns other people and external ceremonies which even a Jew and a Turk would and objectionable, and yet when it concerns their own old Adam, then they become indulgent interpreters of the Law. May the Lord teach them and us to keep the right proportion in all things.

49. And now I want to present the fundamental reason[19] of our faith, for which we have abolished the elevation of the bread and the cup of Christ. First of all, after having recognized Christ, we have heretofore tolerated the elevation only for the sake of the weaker brethren, so that they would not be frightened away from the Word because of the innovations which they were not yet ready to accept; the natural consequence is, of course, that now, after we have preached the Word sufficiently to them, we also prove by our deeds that God should be served only in spirit with true faith and not with external ceremonies, but on the contrary as regards our actions we should practice those things which are for the good and welfare of our neighbor, and further, that what we believe in our hearts we confirm externally by deed. Moreover, not only to be on guard against evil itself but even against all appearance of evil. Since, then, it has been held that the elevation is a ceremony necessary to the worship of God and a sign that Christ is sacrificed again, which is a most blasphemous error, it should be a detestable matter to all the faithful, even though it is in itself an external matter, and in itself is neither good nor evil, and it would be far better always to avoid it rather than tolerate it. And since they tolerate it for a while until the people

---

[18] *Grund*
[19] *Grund und Ursach*

are properly instructed in the Word and then themselves regard it with disgust, well then, as soon as they have been instructed in the Word of God so that their faith in the Word is strengthened by their example, and the disgust with all ungodly things increases in them, they will naturally abolish all these matters of their own accord.

50. And should not a Christian consider with dislike and horror matters which surely have been invented by the devil and have caused great harm to poor souls, whatever they may be in themselves? God commanded the stoning of an ox which had killed a man, and He commanded not to eat his carrion (Exod. 21:8), even though an ox who has no understanding is considered to be guiltless in this matter. Similarly, although the elevation in itself is an external thing and not evil in itself, and further, since many souls are murdered by observing it, by believing that the priest was sacrificing Christ, and that therefore there was no other better deed which would take away the sins and bring salvation; almost as if Christ had not done enough with his own sacrifice on the cross: even so, it is just and right that such an elevation which has been so blasphemous should be abolished and rejected where it is possible to do so even though it can no longer do any harm, providing this can be done without frightening people away from the Word. We should avoid the blasphemers once they have been warned again and again and should have nothing in common with them, and why should we use the same ceremonies with them which, as we have discovered, have been found to be offensive in so many ways? Therefore, then, as Paul states, since both the sacrifices to the idol and also the idol are nothing in themselves, and since as a Christian he has power over all things, and further since we should not be considered to be or become part of the devil and his company to whom the pagans sacrificed, Paul very gently draws them away from sacrificing to idols. "I do not wish," he says, "that you should be part of the communion with the devil. You cannot drink both the cup of the Lord and the cup of the devil. You cannot participate both in the Lord's table and the table of the devil. Or do we want to defy the Lord? Are we stronger than He? All things are lawful for me, but not all things are useful.

All things are lawful to me but not all things edify. Let no man seek his own, but let every man seek the good of the other" (1 Cor. 10:20–24). "Observe then," he says, "all things are lawful to me," "I have all strength," and afterwards he permits them to take part in the sacrifice to the idols; yet, since it could do harm, he would much prefer that they should not do so: does it not, then, make sense that we too should withdraw and reject the elevation, which has been nothing better than a sacrifice to an idol?

51. He who says that we lift up our Lord God and that we have seen our Lord God in the lifting up of the bread and the cup of the Lord, would he not be an immeasurable offense to both Jew and Turk? And especially since the Scriptures state very clearly and John testifies: "No one has seen God at any time, the only begotten Son who is in the lap of the Father, He has declared it to us" (John 1:18). It is proper to hear about God and to believe in God, but to see God is reserved for the hereafter. It is for this reason that God said to Moses: "No man will live who has seen me" (Exod. 33:20). Why, then, does Paul call Him the invisible God? It had been stated, "the bread, the cup of the Lord", as the Spirit of God calls it in Paul where he says, "As oft as ye eat of this bread and drink of this cup," etc. (1 Cor. 11:26), and where neither in this chapter or 10:16–21, where he talks about this, calls it anything else, just as in the Acts of the Apostles and John 13:26, where it is stated that the dipped piece of bread which Judas took from the Lord was the same kind of bread and is called bread only, and if, as the Lord commanded, it had been received and eaten in remembrance of Him, and if the elevation and adoration had been omitted, a great deal of error and superstition in which many poor souls have now been caught to their damnation, would have been avoided. How could anyone call himself a Christian and permit such an elevation when it could be abolished without great detriment?

52. The Fathers write that the Apostle Thomas said, "My Lord and my God" (John 20:28), when he put his hand into the Lord's side: he saw a human being and believed in God; and not the pupils and the teachers of the Pope

write that it is possible to see only the form and the color, and have tolerated that which is completely contrary to all Scripture, contrary to the old teachers, yes, even contrary to what their own teachers have said: namely, "the Lord God lifted up, I want to see our Lord God," and things like that, and so the Mass-lovers and many other irresponsible people of their own kind have made such ridiculous and stupid statements, namely that there probably had been many priests who took the bread and said, "All right, then, lad, you will become the Lord," and many similar blasphemies of that kind. But that kind of error has been very profitable to them, for they claim to be God-makers and claim to be far and away superior to the Blessed Virgin Mary, for she bore Christ only once, but they create Him daily, and in doing so they blaspheme and revile Him more than anyone else on earth.

53. Furthermore, when this bread and this cup were elevated, the people worshipped them as their God and their Christ as physically present with some strange little prayers; and these really were supposed to be much more powerful than at other times, especially since the true, saving presence of God and Christ is invisible, and possible only through true faith. Otherwise God is here, there and everywhere and fills heaven and earth. In this manner the Pharisees, when they crucified Jesus, saw and touched Him physically, but it was of little use to them. For this reason Paul writes: "Although we have known Christ after the flesh, yet now we know Him no longer" (2 Cor. 5:16). For it is surely true, as Christ Himself says, "It is the spirit which gives life, the flesh is of no use. The words which I speak, they are spirit and life" (John 6:63); in the same way it is essential to listen carefully and to believe the words that the body and the blood of Christ were sacrificed once for all on the cross for our sins and make perfect all the elect, and it is for the proclamation of such a faith that the bread is eaten, and the cup is drunk in remembrance of, and in thanksgiving for, such a salvation, just as Christ said, and the elevation and exhibition which He did not command should be omitted.

54. If that group, the Mass-lovers, had been just as much concerned for the poor souls and the purity of the faith as for their bellies, and if they had read this in the Fathers about Thomas, namely that he had seen one thing and then believed and worshipped something else, seen the human being and worshipped the God, they would have been able to say here, too, "you see one thing, you believe another, and you worship a third"; the bread and the cup can be seen and so the Holy Spirit describes it as such, and surely He would know best how to describe it. It is quite proper to believe that the body and the blood of Christ were sacrificed on the cross once for all for our salvation, but God alone should be worshipped. It is for this reason that Christ always pointed to the Father, even though He was one With the Father, so that no one should be restricted by His humanity. For this reason He called Himself the way and said: "No one comes to the Father except through me" (John 14:6); and Paul, also for this reason, calls Him a mediator between God and men, but according to the flesh, for he says: "There is one God and there is one mediator between God and men, the man Christ Jesus" (1 Tim. 2:5). It follows then that if they had been true servants of Christ they would have pointed from the human, external things to the Spirit and to God.

55. The Lord commanded that we should eat the bread and drink the cup and immediately pointed from the physical to the Spirit, and commanded us to remember Him; but the Papists, on the contrary, by ignoring the memorial of the death of Christ, and this was the only reason for the institution and observance of the Lord's Supper, yes, also by placing the emphasis on the physical seeing and the physical adoration rather than on the partaking, misled the people into believing that, should they see and adore the bread and the cup [of the Lord][20] once a day, they would receive good fortune and salvation on that day, regardless of their manner of life; and I say nothing about the many superstitions which have crept in, in connection with certain little prayers which, spoken at the time of the elevation, were supposed

---

[20] "of the Lord" is not found in D. S.

to have some miraculous powers, as is known to everyone; and further, there are many who believed that, should they offer a penny between the elevation of the bread and of the cup, this would be beneficial, for fever in one place and toothaches in another, and many other superstitions and idolatries have arisen in this connection; just as all people have discovered the truth for themselves: if the root is rotten and idolatrous, how can any good thing spring forth?

56. Therefore my conclusion in this whole matter is: since in the Christian congregation all things should be done for edification, and since we know that the elevation in itself cannot serve to edify, for the reason that the Word of God does not teach it, heretofore, however, as it has been used by the Papists and has brought forth unspeakable harm and destruction of souls, and so far has been tolerated by us whom the Lord has enlightened and sent to proclaim His Holy Gospel, for this reason alone, that the weak masses before they have been instructed by the Word should not be frightened away from the Word through the abolition of the same [elevation] as an innovation which they have not yet been able to recognize as useful and divine; now, however, everyone is able to have a good hope instead and has better knowledge through the daily preaching, so that in a Christian congregation one may and should abolish all human sins, but especially those which have been invented by the Antichrist and used to great and public offense, as has happened with the elevation: so with God and out of faith, we no longer allow or tolerate this elevation, so that no one should think that we desire to have communion with the Antichrist and at the same time not only drink the cup of the Lord but also be partakers of the table of the Lord and the table of the Antichrist, which, of course, is quite impossible (1 Cor. 10:21).

57. As servants of the Spirit we feel compelled to preach constantly that the Spirit gives life but that the flesh is completely useless, so that we lead the people beyond all material things to right faith and love of the Spirit. Therefore, since the Lord instituted nothing physical in His supper except the eat-

ing and drinking alone, and that for the sake of the spiritual, namely as in memory of Him, and since we have observed that many cared neither to consider seriously the physical reception nor the spiritual memorial, but instead, just as before, were satisfied with seeing and material adoration, and that these two things up to now have been held in higher regard than the Word of God: we have, for the sake of such weak and indolent Christians for whom it is always necessary to add to the words also the example of works and deeds, always attempted to remove the physical which was not instituted by God, and therefore up to now had been used to their harm, and by doing so, lead them to the spiritual. And this has also been our experience in regard to the idols and pictures, namely, that many of the people rejected them totally after they had been removed physically.

58. And now we will state the fundamental reasons of our faith,[21] why we have done away with and abolished the elevation of the bread and the cup in the Lord's Supper. He who will allow God to be the Lord and His Word the greatest treasure, will be thoroughly pleased with this action; however, he who considers the inventions of man and superstitious abuses of first importance rather than the words and ordinances of God, him we must abandon as being blind. "God must be obeyed more than man" (Acts 5:29); yes, for the sake of God one must surrender, deny and hate even father, mother, wife, child and all things.

V
Reason Why the Popish Vestments Have Been Abolished

59. At the celebration of the Mass, the priest was required to wear curious vestments; if he did not, it was considered a mortal sin. First a linen cloth on his head, which had a border made of precious material and two long ribbons which he tied around his waist, which they called a humeral. After that a loose linen vestment which must have been too long for the priest,

---

[21] *Grund und Ursach.*

and probably for this reason he had to fold it back, and this too with a linen belt and it, too, below, behind and before was made of precious material, silk or some other expensive cloth, and had two rectangular shields and similarly on the sleeves a cover made of the same material, and this vestment they called an alb. And over all this a long, narrow sash, again made of precious material, which the priest had to put around his neck and then crossed the ends in front of the chest and on each side under the girdle, with which he tied together the alb so that it covered his breast like a Burgundy cross, and this they called a stole. A similar but shorter sash, whose ends were sewn together, hung from his left arm and they called that the maniple or the hand-flag,[22] and over all this he had to wear, suspended from the neck, a covering vestment without sleeves, made of precious material, with an opening at the top for the head and open at both sides; wide in the back and in front, one part somewhat tapered at the bottom, and the other part cut round and somewhat shorter than the alb, and on the center back a cross, in front a border, both ornamented with precious embroidery and pictures.

60. This is the magnificent armor[23] of the Mass-lovers, which I have described in such detail because I have no doubt that in a few years a knowledgeable Christian will be brought, by the Word of God, to the point where he would hardly believe it if he heard that amongst Christians there had ever been such a masquerade. I have not taken the time to describe the armor of the bishops, which was even more foolish, or of the Levites, as they called them, and others like that, which I did not choose to describe, so that the reader should not be distracted from better things by such foolishness. The vestments just described have heretofore customarily been used in our celebration of the Lord's Supper for the reason just stated, in order to retain the good will of the people until they firmly grasp the Word and then abolish them along with other Papist ceremonies, for the usefulness and edification

---

[22] *Handfan*
[23] *Rustung* - like a knight's armor.

of the people. For before the Word of God is heard and believed, such abolition would be of little use. To the unbelievers all things are impure, just as contrariwise all things are pure to the faithful. We hope, therefore, that the faithful will forgive us for retaining such vestments and understand that since the Lord has revealed His Word to us, we have not regarded such things as necessary nor retained them in order to win favor with God, but only for the sake of the inexperienced, so that we would not frighten them away from the Word through innovations which they could not understand, and therefore through such external things[24] we try to accommodate ourselves to them.

62. And since it was only for the sake of the inexperienced that we have retained the vestments just described, until they had experienced and were acquainted with the will of God through the Word, and after a great deal of preaching all the lambs of Christ had heard and known the voice of their shepherd, it then became necessary for us, in order to follow and obey it alone, also to give an example by deed. For this reason we have abolished all the vestments described above and in the celebration of the Lord's Supper we use no special vestments but only a choir gown, and the same for preaching the Word, and with this choir gown, which is not specially esteemed and has not been consecrated, we hope to serve visitors and those of our own people who are concerned that things be done decently and in order, in the hope that no one will be neglected because we proclaim the Word of God clearly and diligently.

63. But that mummery which they consider to be highly essential to the Mass, we have no longer tolerated, after diligent and extensive preaching of the Holy Gospel, and especially since we did not think that any useful purpose could be served for anyone, also since we have no doubt that such vestments found their origin in blasphemous pagan use and human invention; for the Holy Scriptures never taught them. Since, then, in our worship

---

[24] *Mitteln* (i. e., *adiaphora*, things indifferent, neither good nor bad in themselves).

of God nothing should be used which would serve idolatry or which has been invented by us, it follows that we should have nothing whatsoever to do with such vestments (Deut. 12:29–32). Further, since their origin was questionable, they were also exploited by the priests to the harm of many. By wearing such vestments they considered themselves to be holier and better than others; but should it happen that in the Mass one little piece was forgotten, it was considered to be a sin, and he considered himself very highly in the sight of God, who entered into the presence of God with washed hands, prescribed prayers, removal of his weapon, combing of the hair, and who in addition dressed himself up in such vestments with spiritual care and reverence. And he was held in such high regard that, should a Christian desire to be baptized and consecrated by a common priest, it was only a bishop who could bless the Mass vestments. And what was most harmful to faith was that such vestments proclaimed that the Mass-maker, the priest, was sacrificing Christ and would use and handle God, whom all Scripture praises as eternally unchanging. And this was considered to be so precious and meritorious a deed to him who wore such vestments, that it made the person of the priest, even though he was an openly practicing adulterer, miser, blasphemer and the dregs of all vice, so holy that he who did not bow down before him nor bow his knees to him, was considered by him to be no Christian at all.

64. All these of course are dreadful and detestable superstitions; there never is any holiness in things themselves, since they wear out through being handled, and no one should have a guilty conscience over that (Col. 2:16). So the Lord rejects all external cleanliness and embellishment; the faith of the heart alone is of value to Him (Matt. 23:23–26). The claim that the priests sacrifice Christ in their Mass is in itself such a damnable error, as we have already shown, that a Christian certainly should deter anything which supports it in any way whatsoever. For he who loves Christ truly and finds delight in His law, will find it impossible to suffer and endure the inventions of the anti-Christ used in the destruction of faith, unless, of course, love and consideration for the weaker brethren force him to do otherwise.

Therefore, if these things can be abolished without undue unwillingness on the part of the weak ones, it should be every Christian's greatest desire to abolish them; just as no one who is true and faithful to his Lord should tolerate or permit those matters which were instigated and used by the enemies of the Lord and to the Lord's displeasure, no matter what they are in themselves. Therefore every true Christian will feel like David, when he said: "I despise lies and find them an abomination, but your law I love" (Ps. 119:163). Lies, however, and vanities do not flow from the Word of God, for if all men be liars and vain, just as Scripture shows everywhere, how could it be possible otherwise than that they would invent lies and vanities?

65. Furthermore, the Mass vestments are not only lying and vainly deceiving inventions, leading to much superstition and error, and have been most harmful and disadvantageous to the purity of the faith, but they have also successfully prevented brotherly love and almsgiving to the poor, and have in addition encouraged ostentation gain and pride. For after the people have been persuaded that it was part of a proper service of worship to maintain and embellish the Mass, everyone was then inclined to want to have that kind of service, since it is human nature to be inclined to depart from the law of the Lord and accept lies, and this has ever been so since the beginning of the world. That result has been that many ignore it that the Lord will say on that day to the goats on the left hand: "Depart from me, you accursed ones, into the eternal fire prepared for the devil and his angels. I was hungry and you did not feed me, I was thirsty and you did not give me drink, I was a stranger and you did not receive me into your home, I was naked and you did not clothe me, I was sick and in prison and you did not visit me." And should they say that they did not see the Lord suffer any of these things, He will answer them: "Truly I say to you, what you have not done, to one of the least of my brethren you have not done to me" (Matt. 25:41–45). Yes, this dreadful judgment of Christ is ignored: that which should be given to the least of them is regarded as if it had been lost, and yet it is given to the Lord alone and is pleasant in His sight; but instead of that they give pieces of gold, velvet, damask and other silks with all sorts

of precious materials so that the priests masquerade in them, and rascals or knaves are considered to be saints, and the superstition, covetousness and mischievousness of the anti-Christ are supported and strengthened.

66. Yes, it has come to this, that such great pride, ostentation and knavery with precious vestments has been customary with lords and children of the world by making Mass vestments out of the precious cloth, which is indeed a work of the devil, and encourages them to spiritual malice and blasphemy, and what is worse, they believe all along that God is being paid and repaid for all things. And so memorial plaques are attached so that everyone can see who is the donor, and they are really nothing but decoys, since the children of Adam by nature are hungry for praise, so that every fool, in order to imitate them, gives something too; and if he can't afford to do very much he will at least pay part on a Mass vestment as long as he is permitted to put his nameplate on it, and when the nobility observe their anniversaries, priests must observe the Mass in the Mass vestments donated by them. And who can enumerate all the stupidities, superstitions, and annoyances which find their source in such mummery and are even supported by it? The planting is not by the Father, so how can you expect it to bring forth good fruit?

67. Since with us all things should edify, that is, they should encourage faith in the one and only Christ, and that it is from Him alone that we expect all good things, and love for our neighbor as for ourselves, and be concerned about him; and since there is no doubt that the Mass vestments harm and do not encourage either faith or love, and in many other ways are offensive, we have quite simply abolished them after the divine Word has become common property among us, unlike those others who have been blinded by God so that they do not desire to hear it and are frightened away by the disregard of the Word, and consequently are counted with the goats and not the lambs of Christ; and for this reason it is absolutely essential neither to suffer nor to permit such things.

68. And no one should use as a rejoinder the example of the use of vestments by the high priests in the Law (Exod. 28). "For we should no longer deal with shadows, since we have the true body of Christ" (Col. 2:17). We should no longer cling to the physical ordinances (Gal. 4:8–9; Col. 2:8, 16), if we desire to serve God in spirit and in truth (John 4). Christ is our High Priest in the line of Aaron, and just as He did not enter into the Holy of Holies made with hands, which is a reflection of eternal things, but into heaven itself to appear before the face of God (Heb. 9:24); even so His priestly garments, and those of all of us who are united with Him in true faith and therefore are also priests, are not made with hands, but spiritual clothing such as truth, justice and righteousness and all things which are in Christ; for all those who have been baptized have put on Christ (Gal. 3:27).

69. For there is a tremendous difference; the Jews had priestly vestments and priests and many officiants, but this was according to the command of God, and from among all the people it was only Aaron, with his sons and their descendants: but with us many unqualified persons have proclaimed themselves as *sacerdotes,* that is, "sacrificers," and have on their own invented curious vestments, but God Himself knew nothing concerning this. The Scriptures teach us everywhere that we should consider spiritual and eternal what the Jews considered to be physical and temporal. Therefore, just as they had Aaron, a physical, temporal officiant who entered into the physical Holy of Holies with physical adornment and offered sacrifice in a physical way, etc., we on the other hand now have a spiritual, eternal and high officiant robed with the clothing of salvation, of righteousness and glory, who sacrificed Himself once and for all, which has eternal validity to perfect all the saints; we are now, through faith, officiants with Him, for we are one with Him, and with each other. "In Christ Jesus there is neither Jew nor Greek, neither slave nor free man, neither male nor female, but we are all together one" (Gal. 3:28). Just as He sacrificed Himself once and for all, we too should surrender our bodies as a sacrifice along with our sacrifices of praise and thanksgiving. For this no physical adornments are necessary.

70. It is about such officiants, that is, of all true Christians who are the beloved bride of Christ, that David sings: "The king's daughter is indescribably beautiful inwardly, her raiment is wrought gold, she shall be brought before the king in embroidered clothing" (Ps. 45:14–15), if the inner man is properly adorned with true faith and love, it will shine forth outwardly, it will shine with the gold of divine wisdom and all sorts of mercies and virtues; and this is the marriage garment which all those should wear who come to the marriage feast of Christ, otherwise they will be thrown into the outer darkness. All of us should strive after such adornment, just as we are all one in Christ and are God's *sacerdotes,* that is his officiants, and should leave external things to the children of the world. When such things are used in the Old Testament they are merely images and shadows of the real things (Heb. 7:23–2, 8; 8:5).

71. Finally, whatever is done in a Christian congregation should be done in such a way that Christians learn thereby to despise physical splendor and adornments. Since all things had to be decorated with gold, silver, precious stones and silk, such pride and ostentation should be despised all the more. The pagans realized that such ornamentation disgraced God more, as if we wanted to show that God, like us, had the desire for gold and similar stupidities, but He is a spiritual, eternal prize and gives heavenly and eternal treasures to His own, and adorns them with spiritual ornaments.

72. In conclusion, and with this I come to the end of this section, the Lord's Supper is nothing less than a sacrifice, as has been indicated often enough above, and in addition it is a ceremony of the New Testament, wherein all things should have a spiritual orientation. Therefore there is no place here for the adornment and the embellishments of Aaron. All these were only pictures and shadows of spiritual things, and we should deal with them now in such a way. Christ observed the Lord's Supper in ordinary clothing and so did His beloved apostles; why then should we employ much adornment and prettily decorated clothing? Therefore we hope that all the

elect of God will be pleased that we have abolished the Papist mummery which has been of little use and has caused much harm.

VI
Why the Prayers and the Gestures Used by the Priests Have Been Abolished and Changed, and Further, Why the Table Called Altar Has Been Displaced

73. The Mass books contain all sorts of prayers and words, but especially those which they call the minor and the major canon, which deal with the sacrifice as if Christ were sacrificed by the priest, which is such a horrid, corrupt error; in addition they use such misleading, poisonous words, over and above any found in the Holy Gospels, and those which were read from the Holy Scriptures in the Mass, and it was considered a great sin if a few words were omitted or if the words were not recited in the right order; and if they did read words from the Gospels or any other part of the Scriptures, it did not matter at all how they were read, but they were mumbled and jumbled together in any old way. Therefore, since such prayers and words in themselves were wrong and misleading and could lead to nothing but superstition and disregard of divine words and truths, and this, of course, is quite obvious and undeniable, and since we have resolved to say nothing in the Christian congregation unless it edifies, we have for some time abolished the Canon and those prayers which were not in harmony with the Holy Scriptures. The Canon and many other prayers in the Mass contain godless, misleading words, completely contrary to Holy Scripture; everyone who knows Christ and reads for himself will recognize this. This has been very clearly stated by the highly blessed Ulrich Zwingli, the apostle of Zurich,[25] in a little book dealing with the Canon and printed recently. So there is no need for me to say too much about that at this time.

---

[25] *"De canone missae epicheresia"* (C. R. Zw 2, 552–608).

74. In the Mass itself it has been customary to use many strange gestures such as bowing, making the sign of the cross, kissing, beating the breast, raising and lowering the hands, turning away from and toward the people, and it was considered a dreadful sin if anyone omitted such gestures which they themselves called shadowboxing,[26] or executed them in the wrong way. For this reason it took a tremendous effort on the part of the young priests to master them; and he who knew how to perform them well was considered a devout, spiritual priest by the others, and the dear, little, old ladies loved to have him officiate, and paid him to read the Mass for them. This quite obviously meant a violation of both faith and love, that is, of the total Christian life: of faith because it was believed contrary to all Scripture, that one showed God a favor by such buffoonery, for if such performances were not supposed to be a service to Him, it would not have been considered a sin either to omit something or not to perform it properly.

75. Now, it is exactly against this that Jesus speaks: "God is a spirit and desires that He should be worshipped in spirit and in truth" (John 4:23, 24). For when Christ says that God should be served and worshipped in spirit, they say that he should be served and worshipped with physical gestures, and when He desires that they should pray to him in truth, they teach [people] to mock God with pretense and hypocrisy. For who would not think it a mockery if someone proclaimed great love with lovely words, smiling, embracing and things like that, and knew deep down in his heart that he was his enemy? Who would not deride it as a mockery if women were to lament greatly, howl and wring their hands over their heads and act as if in their great sorrow they would faint dead away, but did not feel it deep in their hearts? Therefore the manner in which the priests carry on at the altar is nothing else but pure mockery and hocus-pocus: there they drop to their knees, look up to heaven, beat their hands together, knock on their breasts, let out howls as if they were full of remorse and pain over their sins, but while they lament, reel and bow, their eyes fasten on frivolous women, they

---

[26] *Schirmstreiche.*

make secret signs to them, while the congregation concentrates on the sacrifice; is there need to say anything more? Everyone can see quite clearly from their whole life, behavior, words and conduct before and after the Mass, just how seriously they take it. A miserable penny is able to produce in them such devotion and sorrow. How is it possible for anyone to endure such a person performing such hocus-pocus in front of him, yet knowing that his heart is so far away; surely God, who is eternal truth, and who constantly condemns hypocrisy, everywhere, would consider such a spectacle with disgust and the highest annoyance.

76. To be sure, when the heart is full of devotion, love for God, or remorse, it will find expression in external gestures, but it will be an outward expression of an inward devotion, love or remorse. I would as little presume to prescribe how anyone should laugh for joy and jump for joy when he had no joy in his heart, as I would teach anyone how to express devotionally and sorrowfully his inner devotion and remorse. Therefore, to make rules and regulations about such gestures which are made in the same manner by all of them, when most of them have neither love for God nor true remorse, can give rise to nothing else than the purest hypocrisy, hocus-pocus and blasphemy; it is far better for him who desires to be a Christian, to ignore these things and to allow the spirit to have free reign, so that he will act and be exactly as his heart is moved to devotion and remorse and this will be of great benefit to the congregation of God. What else would God say to such mocking pomp of the godless than what He said to the similar hypocrisy of the Jews? "Should you lift up your hands, I will turn away my eyes, and should you multiply your prayers, I will not listen" (Isa. 1:15). Similarly He says through Joel that they should rend their hearts and not their garments, which was indeed a gesture of those who repented (2:13), but many practiced it with false hearts. God is truth, therefore He requires that nothing shall be undertaken except in truth, and that we be sincere in all things. And David also says: "I will go up into Thy house because of Thy great

goodness and worship toward Thy holy temple in Thy fear" (Ps. 5:8).[27] Where there now is the fear of God, who destroys the liar and hates all hypocrites, no one to be sure will presume to mock God, but will speak with David, and this in truth: "I will give thanks to Thee from my whole heart in the council of the righteous and in the congregation" (Ps. 111:1).

77. Therefore, it is now evident that the pomp of the Mass, the bowing and scraping, looking up and looking down, beating hands together and other gestures, are harmful to faith in three ways: first, many poor priests are convinced that by doing so they do God a special favor, even though He requires only the spirit. Next, their consciences are bound with such poor elements, that is, external ordinances, that they feel bound to confess and fear their sins against them. Thirdly, although such actions are not done from the heart but with vain pretense and therefore slander and mock God deeply, one has no fear of the sinfulness of such action but believes that a service is rendered to God.

78. Love is greatly harmed because through such pretensions to apostolicity[28] the simple minded are deceived and are led to contribute at the expense of the poor, but to the advantage of some cowardly, loose-living bellies, who by their lives not only vex the whole congregation of God, but also rule and live in pomp. Since, then, such gestures are harmful and useless, yes, they are even unable to be believed by all without mocking God, and in no way can lead anyone to devotion, love and remorse, they cannot and must not continue to be observed by Christians as has been customary. Since, then, we have been redeemed from such external ordinances through the blood of Christ, and since no one should bind the conscience of anyone with these things, even those which were commanded by God to the old Fathers, is it justifiable to allow the observance of such poisonous, false and hypocritical inventions which are observed without any kind of justification in

---

[27] The reference should read Verse 7, not 8.
[28] *Apostutzlerei*

the Word, but even completely contrary to the Word of God? It is for this reason that we had to abolish them, and give all the people the example of serving God in those things alone which He had commanded, and to do so in spirit and in truth.

79. And if someone should say that making the sign of the cross is of such ancient usage that Tertullian 1300 years ago wrote that it was customary for Christians to make the sign of the cross on the forehead, whatever they did or began to do: concerning this custom read the book by the same teacher, *De Corona Militis*; and for this reason it should not be abolished. Reply: the death of Christ, suffered on the cross, is our salvation, and such remembrance and sign remind us that we should remain firm in our faith in God, and strengthen us to bear our cross more courageously, and therefore are by no means to be rejected. However, signs are signs and should remain signs and it should in no way be admitted that the signs are what they signify. Therefore, if anyone, as was done at the time of Tertullian, makes the sign of the cross on his forehead or anywhere else, each time before or after some action, and in so doing calls to remembrance the death of Christ, so that he would do or not do all things in an unhindered faith in God, thinking at all times how dearly he was purchased from his sins; so that he would die to sin under all circumstances and thus submit himself to the cross, so that he can say with Paul: "Far be it from me to glory in anything except in the cross of our Lord Jesus Christ, through which the world was crucified for me and I to the world" (Gal. 6:14); surely he should be punished in no way, for without any doubt the Fathers reminded themselves in the same manner of the cross of Christ, and found it pleasant to sign themselves with the sign of the cross, so that they should not be ashamed of it but freely take their cross upon themselves and follow bravely in the footsteps of their Lord; and to do this they were encouraged daily.

80. In our time, however, a special power has been ascribed to the sign: it is claimed that it exorcises devils, blesses all things, gives a happy beginning to all things; but all these things are given to the faithful through the death

of Christ. For this reason it has come about that the wood which is claimed to be and is worshipped as part of the cross of Christ has been mounted in silver and gold, and so that the people may earn substantial indulgences, they are allowed to kiss it. After that many other crosses appeared, bleeding crosses, crosses which descended from heaven, crosses which came from purgatory — in all these an unbelievable amount of superstition and offense are caused and maintained; I will remain silent concerning the many superstitious blessings and spells which are encouraged by the holy signs. This was the natural consequence of ascribing too much significance to the sign, while at the same time we have ignored within our hearts that which the sign signifies, namely the death of Christ, so that we should rather have desired to accept it in faith and become like Him.

81. But since we have not understood what the cross of Christ or our cross really means or is able to do for us, God has decreed, because of our great ingratitude, that we should over-emphasize the sign and reject the right thing, the real meaning of the sign, that we should prefer the shadow to the reality, and that we should reject both the cross of Christ and our own cross. For, since we have been redeemed, sanctified, consecrated and blessed through the cross of Christ, that is through His death alone, we have substituted, instead, the sign of the cross made with hands; especially so if it was made by priests or high dignitaries; thereby the knowledge and the power of the cross of Christ have been nullified. Similarly, if God has given us a cross to bear, illness or other things, or has blessed us in some other ways, many have made the sign of the cross in order to ward off the cross of the Lord, when instead such a sign should have admonished or encouraged us bravely to bear the cross which the Lord wanted to lay upon us. Such misuse and superstitious belief regarding this sign (and there are so many of them that it would be impossible to list half of them) have been instrumental in making a ceremony out of it, and in prescribing precisely where and how many times the sign of the cross should be made; the immediate result was that people were mortally afraid if they did not make the sign of the

cross very diligently. This again gave rise to the error that the sign had a peculiar power, namely, that they felt compelled to use it fervently in the Mass and all blessings, and consequently one superstition grew out of another, until no one knew the meaning of the cross of Christ, or our cross, or why such signs were used in the first place and why they are still in use, and how they should be used correctly.

82. Since, then, such ceremonies have been introduced without any justification in the Word and have given rise to much superstition, we have abolished them also, with this concession, that should anyone desire to use such a sign, since in itself it is an external thing, he is free to use it; but we have taught that such freedom should be employed only for the growth of the congregation of God, and how it could be used in a Christian way; about this we have spoken briefly above. We hope, further, since we must be examples of both Christian freedom as well as other good actions—for many believed they were not bound to these matters or that these things were indifferent to them, and yet could not reject them without scruples of their conscience (when they came right down to it)—we hope, then, that the faithful will not hold it against us that we have made some changes in matters concerning Mass gestures and the sign of the cross which the priests themselves, who are nothing more than scoffers, call shadowboxing.[29] And even though all of us were so filled with faith that we would not need such examples, we should feel free to make use of all things; further, since such pomp is at all times a devilish thing, full of mockery, and does not have a good origin, and has encouraged a tremendous amount of error: how could Christians, who in all things attempt to seek the purity of the faith and whatever will further it, not consider it to be a detestable thing?

83. In addition to this, when the opportunity presented itself, we have erected tables in some of our churches, so that in the celebration of the Lord's Supper the minister would face the people. The reason for doing this was

---

[29] *Schirmstreiche.*

that in a Christian congregation all things should be done decently and in order, and if the congregation prays and gives thanks, it is best that it be done in such a way that everyone can reply with "Amen" (1 Cor. 16:26), and for this reason we have ordered that in all congregations all things should be sung and read in the German language, we will say more about this later on; and since the opportunity presented itself for all people to understand all the words of the prayers and thanksgiving, we have again, with great fervor, made use of our Christian freedom, so that the superstitions in connection with the consecrated altars, which only the bishops were allowed to consecrate at great expense, should be energetically abolished, since we have only one altar, one sacrifice and one priest—all these are Christ—and since Paul speaks about a table of the Lord and nowhere mentions an altar (1 Cor. 10:21). Since, then, altars were a hindrance both to faith and to love, and since many unnecessary expenditures were made on them which should have been given to the poor, and since such abolition will serve many good purposes, there is no doubt about it that every Christian will be delighted to help and approve of this. The Papists considered it essential to pray facing the rising sun: but it is only necessary to pray in spirit and in truth, and time and place are of little consequence, and so among us we believe that it is completely inconsequential in whatever direction we face when we pray, as long as the heart is turned to God; for this reason we think it is quite proper to prove such freedom with our actions.

VII
Why the Lord's Supper is Held Only on Sundays in the Presence of the Congregation

84. It has been customary of late to hold the Mass several times daily, especially when payment was involved, even though no one wanted to have anything to do with the priest of the Lord's table; we know, however, that the Lord's Supper is a bond of Christian community through which we, like Christ, that is through Him and for His sake, have all things in common, and so it has been customary with us to observe the Lord's Supper only on

Sundays when the whole congregation partake together with the minister. Christ Himself observed it in His congregation and offered all of them the bread and the cup, saying, "All of you, drink of it" (Matt. 26:27). Similarly Paul instructed his Corinthians to observe the Lord's Supper when the congregation assembled (1 Cor. 11:20). And "The cup of blessing which we bless, is it not the communion of the blood of Christ? The bread which we break, is it not the communion of the body of Christ? For we who are many are one bread and one body when we all partake of one bread" (10:16–17).

85. It can be seen clearly from these words that the Lord's Supper should never be observed for one person alone, but should be observed by all disciples of Christ in the congregation. By doing this they should recall that they are all sinners together and are damned together, but that they have been saved through the offering of the body of Christ and the shedding of His blood on the cross; so that they further confess that Christ does not belong to any one of them but to all; through it they also have true communion of the body and the blood of Christ, and are one body and one bread; from this it further follows that all Christians believe together that they have been saved through the offering of the body and the shedding of the blood of Christ and that both spiritual and worldly people eat and drink the flesh and the blood of Christ (John 6:53–56), so that they also all together partake of the table of Christ, which is a memorial and a thanksgiving for such salvation, through which faith in God is strengthened and love to all men is rekindled and refreshed, but first of all to the members of the household of faith.

86. In compliance with the Word of God we have abolished all fast days except Sunday, and the reason for this I will give later on; and so the whole congregation assembles together only on Sundays and we observe the Lord's Supper at that time only, so that some of the members of the congregation, together with the priest, may receive the bread and the cup of the Lord. For neither good work nor sacrifice is accomplished for the congregation by one person, as the lying Papists have said, but as Paul calls it, by one

communion. This name has remained in Greek and Latin, the last collects together point towards this too, nor has the deception of the anti-Christ been successful in rendering it of less esteem than this anywhere else. Yes, it did happen that if a brother and sister[30] wanted to partake together at the table of the Lord, they celebrated the Mass earlier, almost as if the lay people should have no part in it, and then they were given only the bread of the Lord and not the cup; and thereby many of them were robbed of the communion of the blood. For as Paul says: "The cup which we bless is the communion of the blood of Christ."

87. Now there are some truly pious men, well versed in Scripture who prefer that the Lord's Supper should be observed rarely, and that at those times the whole congregation of Christ should observe it together.[31] They have given good justification for their opinion by citing certain Scripture passages. For the Lord Himself observed it in his manner by commanding them to drink all together out of the cup, and there is no doubt about it that all ate the bread together, too. And, therefore, in such an observance of the Lord's Supper they recalled the death of Christ and were thankful: why then should not all Christians observe it together, since together they have been redeemed by it?

88. In addition, there are some people who are fearful of participating in the Lord's table because they believe, and they are fearful because of old erroneous belief, that they are not good enough or worthy enough, in spite of the fact that the only requirement [for participation in] the Lord's Supper is that one should believe he has been redeemed by the death of Christ, and desire only to be strengthened by God in such a faith, and in love for the neighbor. This is the interpretation which every Christian should hold when he goes to the Lord's Supper as often as it is served, and if he does not hold this interpretation, then he is not a true Christian, and even though he

---

[30] Of an order.
[31] Does he mean, for example, Zwingli?

mingles in the congregation of Christ and wants to be considered a Christian, at the same time he despises the body of the Lord, since he pretends to be a member, or at least he pretends to have a far better Christian disposition than he really has, and again at the same time is guilty of the body and blood of Christ, especially since he congregates[32] with other Christians at this memorial, and wants others to think that he believes that the body and blood of Christ were given for him. They believe further that it would be a good thing for the whole congregation to celebrate the Lord's Supper together, so that we can reestablish the Christian ban, whereby those who through their actions have proven themselves to be un-Christian, should be kept not only from the Lord's Supper, but from the communion of Christians, until the Lord would grant them repentance and the grace to lead a good life.

89. We proclaim, therefore, that it is in greater harmony with Christian institution and the custom of the ancient Church and in many other ways useful, that all of us who want to be considered Christians and should be one bread and one body, ought not to be reluctant to partake together of one bread; and since all of us believe that the Lord gave His body and blood for all of us, so all of us together should be diligent to show forth our communion through the Lord's Supper. But in spite of this, since many consider the Lord's Supper to be an external matter which by itself is not essential, we found it difficult to encourage the people to take it more seriously, so that the previous superstitions that such a supper would make them devout or saved should not be strengthened or planted anew. Be this as it may, and since there have always been some who desired to partake of the Lord's Supper with us (God only knows whether it is our fault or their weakness in faith) we have not had the heart to refuse them; however, we have instructed them in the correct usage most diligently.

---

[32] *ursach*

90. Therefore, since the time of the apostles, when the congregation of Christ assembled and observed the Lord's Supper, we, too, have followed that custom of assembling every Sunday, however, for the time being, with some partaking instead of the whole congregation, until such time as the Lord should lead us further through His Word and reform us completely. For since it is an external thing, without which it is quite possible to be saved, we were undecided whether to reject those who desired it or to force others to it; but like the old Fathers, we allowed them to participate and continued to instruct them, even those who had not been received into the fellowship of baptism. Therefore we give thanks to God that He has given our people a heart to hear His Word, which is the best and most necessary thing and which, without any doubt, will instruct them in the future concerning those things which are right and necessary.

91. In the beginning of the Christian Church, more than with us, the Lord's Supper was observed by the whole congregation and there were three reasons for it. The first, no one received baptism and was received into the congregation, unless he completely surrendered himself to the Word of Christ; in our congregation, however, many listen to us preach, but have not surrendered themselves completely to the Word of God, unless they are first brought to a rebirth in Christ. Next, they observed the ban, with which they excluded those who did not live or teach properly; we, however, have to put up with a hodgepodge situation. Thirdly, in those days the Christians were not led astray into a wrong concept of the Lord's Supper, whereas now so much error has been spread by the Papist riffraff, that we think it would be the best thing, wherever the preaching of the Word has been started and whenever it can be done fittingly, to discourage the people from partaking for a little while, until, through the Word, they have a better understanding of the correct usage.

92. Here, then, I have stated the reason[33] why we never observe the Lord's Supper by itself, and therefore celebrate it on Sundays. Whoever desires that we should do more, namely that we should not observe it except in the presence of the whole congregation, and that we should exercise the Christian ban against all those who live improperly, should pray to God to help us in this and other matters, to perfect us, and not hold it against us, that until such a time as the whole congregation, whose good opinion the brothers desire, have reached such a common understanding of the Lord's Supper and to serve those who desire it for all, and observe it with them instead of the whole congregation. It is not unusual that not everyone is able to have a clear understanding concerning external matters, nor is able to be encouraged to observe them correctly, especially since the Church of the apostles at times stumbled around quite badly in matters like this.

93. But the basic justification for our actions in this is that we do not want to injure Christian freedom in regard to the Lord's Supper as in all external matters, nor give anyone cause for false hypocrisy by doing what is not in his heart, and for this reason we wait and force no one, until God should give all one heart and one soul, to continue steadfastly and consistently in the Apostles' teaching and in the communion and in the breaking of the bread and in prayer, in the meantime we welcome those who desire it; for to force them to wait for others would be contrary to our Christian freedom. To reserve it for us alone, however, would be against His institution, His intention, use and name. It is for this reason that such misuse, namely the belief that the Lord's Supper in and by itself is a good work and sacrifice, has arisen from the devilish error of the anti-Christ.

---

[33] *grundtlich Ursach.*

VIII
The Manner in Which the Lord's Supper is Observed Now

94. Up to this point I have described and given the reasons[34] why we have changed and abolished some parts of the Lord's Supper such as: the name Mass, the elevation, Mass vestments, peculiar gestures, repeatedly making the sign of the cross, the use of consecrated altars removed from the people, and that we have observed it not only sometimes but always with the assembled congregation of God and therefore only on Sundays. Now I will very briefly describe what we have retained and also give the reasons[35] for that; for a lot of lies have been spread [about us].

95. When the congregation assembles on Sundays the minister[36] admonishes them to confess their sins, to pray for pardon, and he makes confession to God on behalf of the congregation, and declares the absolution of sins to the faithful; following which the whole congregation sings some short psalms or a song of praise. After that the minister[37] prays a short prayer and reads to the congregation some sections of the writings of the Apostles and gives a very brief explanation of the same. Following this the congregation again sings the ten commandments or something else; after this the priest[38] reads the Gospel and preaches the sermon proper; then the congregation sings the articles of our faith; then the priest prays for those in authority and for all people, and especially for the presently assembled congregation in which he prays for growth in faith and mercy [and love][39] and to observe the remembrance of the death of Christ with fruitfulness. Then he admonishes those who plan to participate in the Lord's Supper with him, that they should do so in remembrance of Christ, that they should die to their sins, should bear their cross willingly, should love their neighbor in truth and should be

---

[34] *ursach*
[35] *grundt*
[36] *diener*
[37] *diener*
[38] *priester*
[39] in D. S. only

strengthened in faith; this must happen when with a faithful heart we realize the immeasurable mercy and kindness which Christ has shown to us in sacrificing His body and His blood to the Father on the cross for us. After this admonition he proclaims the Gospel concerning the Lord's Supper as it is described in the three evangelists: Matthew 26:26-28, Mark 14:22-24 and Luke 22:19-20, as well as Paul, 1 Corinthians 11:23-25. After this the priest distributes the bread and the cup of the Lord among them and partakes of it himself. Then the congregation once more sings a song of praise; after that the minister concludes the Lord's Supper with a short prayer, blesses the people and lets them depart in the peace of the Lord. This is the manner and the custom according to which we now observe the Lord's Supper only on Sundays.

96. Our Scriptural reason and justification[40] are as follows: the beginning of the Christian life should be a confession that all our actions are sinful. For this reason John the Baptist, Christ and the apostles started their sermons with this word: "Repent" (Matt. 3:2; 4:17; Acts 2:38), and in the assemblies of God the confession of sins has always taken first place, with the Fathers it even took precedence over baptism, for it was customary to baptize adults (only)[41] and not children. This is why we begin our service of worship with a common confession of sin and prayer for pardon. As David says, "For this the holy ones will pray before Thee at the proper time"(Ps. 32:6).

97. And again Paul says, "When you assemble, everyone has a psalm, a teaching, a revelation and an interpretation on this and that" (1 Cor. 14:26). The Apostle, therefore, in writing to the Corinthians in this chapter, informs us that when the congregation of God assembles there are teaching, songs of praise, and prayer. And for this reason we have established that instruction, namely concerning both Law and Gospel, should be given in our assembly, and admonitions added thereto; and along with it psalms and

---

[40] *grund und ursach*
[41] only in D. S.

songs of praise should be sung to the praise of God and for the strengthening of faith; and thirdly, prayers for those in authority and for all men, following the teaching of the same Apostle (1 Tim. 2:1–2).

98. Finally, we observe the breaking of the bread and the communion of the Table of the Lord: in this we also follow the teaching of Paul (1 Cor. 11:23–26); all this we conclude properly with thanksgiving, since the Lord Himself concluded His Supper in the same manner (Matt. 26:30). In all these things we desire to follow gladly the example of those of whom it is written, "But they continued steadfastly in the apostles' teaching and in the communion and in the breaking of the bread and in prayer" (1 Cor. 14:26) [Acts 2:42].

99. At this point, I suppose, since Dr. Carlstadt and others have recently raised the question whether the Lord's Supper is only bread and wine, or whether the physical body and blood of Christ are present in it, the reader may expect an explanation from us concerning these matters. Since our brother and co-worker, Wolfgang Capito, has done so in a little book[42] entitled: *What One Should Believe and Reply Concerning the Disputes Between Martin Luther and Andreas Carlstadt*, I want to say a few words about this, for there are some who are horrified concerning these questions, and others would like to blow them up out of all proportion.

100. Therefore those who love the Lord know that we are most anxious to lead the people from the flesh, from physical elements, to the Spirit and spiritual practices, through which faith is strengthened and becomes active through love and good works. For just as God is a spirit, He requires that those who worship Him should worship Him in spirit and in truth. As Paul says "God has enabled us to be the servants of the New Covenant, not of the letter of the Law but of the spirit" (2 Cor. 3:6), So, then, we admonish the people that, since through the death of Christ we have died to all physical ordinances, and since we have received from the Lord only two physical

---

[42] Walch, Vol. XX, No. 9, columns 340 -351, written in fall, 1524.

ceremonies and signs, namely Baptism and the Lord's Supper, they should be more concerned about why He instituted these rather than what they are in themselves.

101. Doesn't the Lord say in the Supper (concerning Baptism we will speak later on below), when He took the bread, gave thanks, broke it and gave it to His disciples: "Take, eat, this is my body which is broken for you, this do in remembrance of me" (1 Cor. 11:24–25)? Should we not, then, eat the bread and drink the cup in remembrance of Him; why then should we quarrel much concerning the bread and wine, rather than think of the death of our Savior and partake with simple faith? Paul writes: "As oft as ye eat this bread and drink of this cup you should proclaim the Lord's death" (1 Cor. 11:26); how, then, can we have quarrelsome disputations concerning the bread and the cup?

102. Even as a father bequeaths a golden cup to his sons and commands that as often as they drink out of it they should think of him and all the good things he had taught them, that they should live together in unity and honor, and they then started a quarrel about the cup, regarding the material it was made of, or how precious, until they started pulling their hair: should they not be considered ungrateful and evil children, who would have been better off never to have received the cup? Or, to use another illustration, to quarrel about the bread and the wine of the Lord, which should be used for the strengthening of faith and the confirmation of the greatest unity, is the same as if a great lord had given his servants some special clothes and ornaments and had commanded that they should wear these in his honor and memory, by which action he desired to give them a great reward, hoping that they would retain a good friendship amongst themselves: and they forgot all about it and started a quarrel over the gift, by doing which they would anger the lord and they themselves would be divided; would they not be foolish people?

103. But this is exactly what happens among those who start a serious quarrel about the bread and the cup of the Lord. The bread and the cup, no matter what we may think about it, will be completely useless to them unless in faith they recall the death of Christ, through which faith and love are strengthened, and by eating the flesh and drinking the blood of Christ spiritually they would have life eternal; and they disregard all this and it becomes for them a mark of their disunity, when it should be a covenant of the greatest unity; and there is no doubt about it they are guilty of the body and the blood of Christ, and what should be the way to life eternal becomes deadly to them.

104. Jesus says a great deal regarding His body as food and His blood as drink: "It is the Spirit which brings life, the flesh is completely useless" (John 6:63). Why do we quarrel, then, about the physical presence? The words of the Lord, when He says: "take, eat, this is my body; take and drink, that is my blood" (Matt. 26:26–28; Luke 22:20); Paul writes, "This cup is the new Testament in my blood" (1 Cor. 11:25), should remain true just as they are true, and they should rather consider that He says in both, "Do this," that is, eat and drink, "in remembrance of me" (Luke 22:19; 1 Cor. 11:24–25). If this is done, and if there is faith, further physical matters will become secondary, except that one eats the bread and drinks the cup, and immediately thinks of that which is spiritual, namely to consider the death of Christ. This remembrance will become so important without any doubting whatever in every believing heart and all endeavors will be directed to proclaim, to praise and to glorify such a death as [a death for] one's salvation; further to become like Him by dying to sin, by carrying one's cross manfully, and also by showing a sincere love to all men.

105. That is what the Lord desires, and not that we should be concerned about physical matters, for when the Lord says: "Do this in remembrance of me," Paul explains it by writing: "As often as you eat of this bread and drink of this cup you will proclaim the Lord's death until He comes" (1 Cor. 11:26); by this he did not mean, as some say: "Do this in remembrance of

me," that is, change bread into my body, or things like that. He commanded to eat the bread and drink the cup for the purpose of doing this in remembrance of Him; and anyone who is not quarrelsome should see that the words of the Lord are quite self-explanatory.

106. If Dr. Carlstadt had been inclined to treat these words of Christ with reverence, he would not have started such disputations, which for the most part are quarrels about words concerning these external things; he would instead have been much more diligent to point everyone from the physical to the spiritual. And for this purpose, since he is a man well versed in the Scriptures, he would have found enough passages and would not have felt constrained to force and torture the words of the Lord with unjustified reasons[43]; as if the Lord, when He said, "take and eat, that is my body" (1 Cor. 11:24), offered the bread to His disciples, but when He used the little word "that," he pointed to His physical body, to indicate that the bread could not have been crucified for us.

107. In the words which the Lord spoke over the cup, as they are recorded by Luke and Paul, it cannot be denied that "that," *touto* in Greek, meant the chalice and not the physical blood of Christ. For He says the drinking cup, or the chalice in Greek *touto to poterion*, "is the New Testament in my blood," and yet this identical tumbler or cup has not been spilled for us. It is understood that the only true body of Christ is offered for us and is crucified, and the only true physical blood is shed for us once, and neither bread nor wine. But that is no reason why the words of Christ should be tortured, rather it is necessary to teach that the bread should be eaten and the wine should be drunk in such a way that one should in the right manner remember the offering of the body and the blood once for all, so that in this way His body is eaten and His blood is drunk spiritually and truly.

---

[43] *ungegrtlndeten ursach*

108. The words themselves give this meaning when we are told to remember Him and His death. And the same is true with regard to the words which he spoke over the cup "This is my blood of the New Testament" (Matt. 26:28; Mark 14:24); however, Luke and Paul [record]: "This cup is the New Testament in my blood" (Luke 2:20; 1 Cor. 11:25). There is no doubt about it, that when He says, "This is the New Testament in my blood," He is speaking about His physical blood shed once-and-for-all for us on the cross, by which there was established between God and us the merciful, new, eternal covenant, mentioned in all Scripture (Jer. 31:9; 31–34); namely that He is our Father and we are His children (Rom. 8:21–31; Heb. 8:6–13; 9:14; 10:15–18, etc.). Therefore the same blood must be referred to in the words stated in Matthew and Mark, namely: "This is my blood"; similarly when he says: "This is my body."

109. And just as the words: "This cup is a New Testament" must be interpreted to mean it is a sign or symbol of the New Testament which is spiritual; why shouldn't the words about the bread: "This is my body," and in Matthew and Mark concerning the cup: "This is my blood," be interpreted similarly concerning the very same bread and the very same cup as a symbol, memorial sign and significance of the true and only body and blood of Christ, which no longer remain among us in physical form. "I tell you the truth," says Christ (John 16:7), "It is better for you that I depart," and Paul, too, no longer recognizes Christ according to the flesh (2 Cor. 3).[44] The same kind of speech is recorded in Genesis, where God describes the circumcision as "His covenant" between Him and Abraham, and calls it a "sign of the Covenant" (17:10, 13).

110. And should someone say: "It seems to me that when the Lord Himself said: 'Do this in remembrance of me' (Luke 22:19), and when Paul says: 'As often as you eat of this bread and drink of this cup you shall proclaim the Lord's death' (1 Cor. 11:26), that this bread and this cup are symbols and

---

[44] So given in Walch; D. S. quotes correctly: 2 Corinthians 5:16.

signs of the sacrifice of Christ offered for us once for all." Well, our quarrel is not over this contention, but whether this bread and cup, in addition to being a symbol and memorial sign of the death of Christ, also signifies His physical body and His physical blood or simply bread and wine.

111. Reply: you have heard that Christ says, "The flesh is of no use"; why then do you ask about the flesh? If you could recognize it as a symbol and sign and accept it with true faith that He gave and sacrificed His body and blood on the cross once for all for your salvation: then you would truly partake of the true body and the true blood of Christ and have eternal life. If, however, you should not receive and use the bread and the cup in this manner: then you would be guilty of the body and the blood of Christ and you would dishonor such a glorious remembrance. Whatever is physical will be of no help to you; if, however, you could accept the spiritual, it would bring you eternal life.

112. Therefore ignore all the other questions; the words are true: "This is my body, this is my blood." Thus the Spirit of God speaks truly through Paul, so that he says: "this bread, the cup." Therefore, accept both of them as right and true; be concerned only with this, that what you receive you receive in memory of the Lord, so that you through faith receive the flesh and the blood of Christ spiritually, that is, believe without any reservations whatsoever that through such a sacrifice you have been delivered from all evil and have been made a child of God. Anything else we need to know, God will surely reveal to us.

113. *Summa summarum:* hold fast to the words of the Lord and do not do violence to them; but remember all the while that the flesh is useless and that everything which is physical here refers to the spiritual. The Lord commands you to eat and drink, that is physical; but the sole purpose is that you should think of Him, believe Him, thank Him and be obedient to Him,

who gave His body and His blood for you. Psalm 22:27[45] refers to this: "The poor shall eat and be satisfied, and they shall praise the Lord who seek Him; your heart shall live forever." Everything must surely agree with this; everything refers to this which is contained in the Holy Scriptures. Dr. Martin Luther, in everything that he has written about this, has always pointed to the Spirit and to faith; and it would have been a good and proper thing if Dr. Carlstadt had never written his devious, envious and foolish words against him.

114. But God grant that there be few in this category, who think too highly of themselves and believe it would be to their disgrace to change their opinions somewhat from those they preached once upon a time, and through which they presume to act vehemently and to embroil further poor consciences, rather than admit they had been in error. God be praised! The high regard in which a person is held has undergone a change: people are no longer inclined to accept certain positions just because a Doctor or preacher or minister said so. If you do not have clear scriptural justification, tread softly, you really need no other persuasive powers. And would to God that, just as we here in Strasbourg have been admonished by Dr. Martin Luther,[46] everyone would be just as concerned to grasp firmly the basic principles, in that case it would be very easy for us to become and to remain united concerning such external matters.

115. That there should be some who claim to throw light from the Law and the Prophets upon the words and work of Christ in the New Testament, that is, to learn from the shadow what the body is really like, and claim to recognize in the hidden face of Moses the clearly revealed face of Christ, and through symbols to proclaim contemporary truth,[47] all this is thoroughly wrong. Moses and the prophets point to Christ; but it is Christ who reveals the face of Moses and the prophets and throws light on them. There-

---

[45] The reference should be to verse 26.
[46] Cf. Luther's "*Vermanung an die Christen zu Strassburg*".
[47] 2 Cor. 3:13–16

fore, since there are some who want to discard the words of Christ in the evangelists and who want to convince people by force concerning the ceremonies of the Law, that is, those who want to ignite the sun, they really accomplish nothing more than to drive the people farther away from them, and confirm them in their opinions.

116. Now, for your further enlightenment: In the Law, those who had sacrificed and were companions of the altar, ate of the sacrifice; therefore, we too must eat of our sacrifice, which is the body and blood of Christ, and therefore the bread of the Lord must be physically His body, and the cup physically His blood; shouldn't, then, Carlstadt say: we should eat of our sacrifice; yes, "He who does not eat the flesh and drink the blood of the Son of Man, he shall in no way have life in Him" (John 6:53). However, these words of our Lord are spirit and life; they must be considered spiritually through faith. Flesh by itself is nothing; and it by no means follows that I should receive this physically in the bread and wine; if that were so, the Law would be spiritual and would be fulfilled with spiritual and not physical matters. Read the epistle to the Hebrews; one symbol does not fulfill another, but spiritual truth is the fulfilling of the symbols. The very fact that we still retain two ceremonies, Baptism and the Lord's Supper, is to some extent according to the Law; just as we are still in part under the Law as long as we are clothed with a sinful body. That which is peculiar to the New Testament and is declared in the Law of Moses and the Prophets is truly a spiritual matter; such as the baptism of Christ through spirit and fire, and the spiritual partaking of the flesh and blood of Christ.

117. Therefore in the name of Christ I admonish all those[48] who feel that they have to write or to preach concerning this matter, to take seriously to heart that they should be servants of the Spirit, not think too highly of themselves, but present the reasons for their faith with gentleness and fear, with sobriety and truthfulness, and all this through the clear words of

---

[48] Does he really mean Carlstadt?

Christ. Otherwise they will surely confuse more and more the consciences of the simple minded who are now able to read the Scriptures for themselves.

118. We believe that we should leave the words in their natural order, but at the same time our thoughts and the thoughts of our listeners should be drawn away from the physical, which the Spirit of God in Paul calls the bread and the cup of the Lord, which naturally should be accepted quite freely, and directed to the spiritual and eternal, namely the once-for-all sacrifice of Christ, by which the saints will be perfected in eternity; and admonish everyone, since the Lord Himself says that the flesh is of no avail, not to cling to the flesh and external things and even less to quarrel with anyone on this account. And besides, we know too that we shall overcome the gates of hell, which, of course, is possible neither for Carlstadt and his repulsive followers nor for some of his opponents. But we are not discouraged, "There must be divisions, so that those who are faithful may be revealed," and in the same way, as always, it is necessary for the Gospel to be attacked and tested on both sides, through enemies and pseudo-friends. Everyone should pray to God with David: "Turn away my eyes so that they do not see vanities; quicken me in Thy way" (Ps. 119:37).

IX
Concerning Baptism

119. Anti-Christ, with his little inventions, has obscured the meaning of baptism, too, even though not quite as much as the Lord's Supper. The worst is that the people are misled into believing that the simple act of baptism would save a child, and should it die unbaptized, it would be unable on that account ever to see the face of God. In addition he (anti-Christ) has overemphasized out of all proportion, chrism, oil, salt, bread, candles and consecrated water, so that baptism was not considered to be complete if any of these were omitted. All this has served to shame and belittle the death of Christ, through which we were sanctified once, as all Scripture teaches.

120. Therefore we felt constrained to preach as the witnesses of Christ, "that through His name all those who believe in Him will receive forgiveness of sins," and have taught, according to the Scriptures, concerning baptism, that there are two kinds of baptism, one by water and one by the Spirit. Christ alone baptizes in the second way, baptism by water was used by John, the Apostles and all the others who baptize. The baptism of Christ, who baptized with the Holy Spirit and with fire, obliterates sin and makes children of God; baptism by water is therefore an external sign. John therefore says: "I baptize you with water to repentance, but He who comes after me is stronger than I...He will baptize you with the Holy Spirit and with fire" (Matt. 3:11), and the Lord Himself says, "John has baptized with water, but you shall be baptized with the Holy Spirit" (Acts 1:5).

121. No one should think it strange that I hold the baptism of John, of the apostles and our baptism to be of equal value, for we also baptize like John and the Apostles, with water. The other baptism, that with the Spirit, Christ has reserved for Himself. And just as John baptized with the baptism of repentance and said to the people that "they should believe in Him who would come after him, that is, in Jesus, that He is the Christ" (Acts 19:4), says to the Jews: "Repent, and everyone be baptized in the name of Jesus Christ for the forgiveness of sins, so you shall receive the gift of the Holy Spirit," that is, admit that you are in need of repentance and be baptized in the name of Christ, that is, with faith that through the name of Christ you will receive forgiveness of sins, and then you shall receive the gift of the Holy Spirit. Note, then, that this is the baptism of Christ with which He baptizes.

122. And should someone say, "Didn't Paul require those in Ephesus, who had been baptized with the baptism of John, to be baptized again in the name of the Lord Jesus, Acts 19:5? How is it possible, then, that the baptism of John and that of the Apostles should be one and the same?" Reply: those were not baptized with the baptism of John but *into* John's baptism or *to* John's baptism. For the Greek says *eis to Joannou baptisma* otherwise they

would have had a greater knowledge of Christ and His baptism, which is done through the Spirit. But Luke writes in the same place, that they said: "We do not know whether there is a Holy Spirit." But John told everyone how "after him would come the One who would baptize with the Holy Spirit and with fire."

123. In Acts 18:24–26 there is a report concerning Apollo, who knew only the baptism of John. Luke writes there that Aquila and Priscilla explained the way of God to him more diligently, but nothing is said (to the elect) that they re-baptized him, and we read nothing like this concerning the apostles either; yes, Christ Himself, who desired to fulfill all righteousness and had received the baptism of the New Covenant, considered the baptism of John to be adequate. By doing so he proclaimed His suffering, through which the sins of the world, which He had taken upon Himself, even though He Himself was without sin, had to be washed away. Furthermore, he confirmed not only the external baptism, but rather much more announced the purpose it should serve and what would follow, should we accept Him with faith and with the fulfilling of all righteousness. For most certainly the Holy Spirit will descend upon us; the Father recognizes us as His beloved children. But immediately we are tested by temptations and sufferings until the sinful body is taken away completely. Neither do we read about the apostles, that they were baptized with any other external baptism. Therefore, it is quite evident that the twelve men in Ephesus, even though they knew nothing of the Holy Spirit, that is, the true baptism of Christ, had not been baptized with the baptism of John but only, as the text; says, *into* the baptism of John, just as if the baptism of water were sufficient in itself. For this reason the Apostle had to point them to Christ and therefore he also allowed them to be baptized into Him.

124. For this reason we know only two kinds of baptism. One with water; John used such a one, the pioneer of the New Testament, the apostles and all Christians. The other is the one with which Christ baptizes through the Holy Spirit and through fire, and this is the same Holy Spirit who destroys

all sins with fire and purifies and refines the inner man like gold. The external baptism by water is nothing but a sign of the inner and spiritual. That is why it is done in the name of Christ or in the name of Father, Son and Holy Spirit; by doing so one points to the faith and hope of the inner baptism which Christ, yes, the Father, Son and Holy Spirit, complete as long as this life lasts; for our sins last just as long.

125. Therefore Paul "all who are baptized in Christ Jesus are baptized into His death, yes, through baptism are buried with Him" (Rom. 6:3–4). For he who is baptized correctly confesses that he is a child of anger, thoroughly unclean, but believes that Christ will cleanse him from all his sins. This is accomplished through the death of Christ, like whom we must become through a daily dying of our old Adam, that is, all our nature. To this he who is baptized surrenders himself; and therefore in him the death of sin will have to be completed; and on account of the certainty of his faith he is already now reckoned as dead and buried with Christ, so that now he is waiting for the new and eternal life. It is on account of this assurance and certainty that the Apostle further says, "As many of you as are baptized, they have put on Christ" (Gal. 3:27). Now it is true there are a lot of dreadful, dirty rags and tatters of the old Adam which still cling to us as long as we live here and are still a long distance away from putting on Christ as our garment: but as long as we believe that it shall come to pass, and in this faith have been baptized in His name, it will surely happen. Therefore it is now our possession through faith, and the Scriptures speak of this.

126. From all this, then, it should be quite clear that the external baptism with water is nothing else than a symbol of the inner spiritual baptism, that is, of the cleansing from all sins, which we must accept in faith, which the spirit of God works in us as long as this life lasts, and which is the true repentance and reform,[49] and the enlightened achieve this faith through baptism. And therefore, to the external baptism we should ascribe the for-

---

[49] As reconstructed in Walch and given in D. S.

giveness of sins as nothing more than a symbol. For the baptism of Christ means the forgiveness of sins, which He accomplishes in the elect through His Holy Spirit.

127. Therefore, as Peter says, "the water in baptism will save us," but right away he explains himself and says: "not the putting away of the filth of the flesh but the covenant of a good conscience toward God through the resurrection" (1 Peter 3:21). Likewise, Paul says, "Christ has cleansed His congregation through baptism with water" but he adds: "with the Word," by which he means the faith, the activity of the Spirit, that is, the inner baptism (Eph. 5:26). In the same way he writes: "He has saved us through the bath of rebirth and renewal of the Spirit," where "the bath" means baptism with water (Titus 3:5). The fact that he immediately adds: "of rebirth and the renewal of the Spirit" shows that he is thinking of the baptism of the Spirit, without which water is water, and baptism is a hocus pocus. The flesh and whatever is physical is of no use in itself.

128. Therefore, if one reads concerning pardon or forgiveness of sins, it should be ascribed to the baptism of Christ. So when Ananias said to Paul: "Arise and be baptized and cleansed from your sins and call on the Name of the Lord," he referred not only to the baptism with water alone, but rather through it to the baptism of the Spirit, which cleanses from sins and gives joy to call upon the Name of the Lord. Therefore it is an insult to Christ and a damnable obscuring of His true spiritual baptism, to say or to mean that the external baptism with water will save, or if this is not done the child will not be saved. It is true, the Lord says: "He who believes and is baptized, he will be saved, but he who does not believe will be damned" (Mark 16:16), but He does not say that whoever is not baptized will be damned. God does not limit His mercy to water.

129. He desired that baptism with water should be a sign, confession, instruction and admonition of His inner baptism. For this reason no one should despise it. No one should build on it, rather than on the baptism of

Christ alone, through which we shall be sprinkled and baptized with the waters of salvation, that is, His Spirit (John 7:38–39). For this reason it is a superstitious foolishness to desire baptism of children before they are born, or to rush baptism in some other awkward manner, as is often done by women facing dangerous births, as if our salvation depended upon mere water. It is far worse that they have been taught to doubt that unbaptized children are saved.

130. This, then, is one of our most significant reforms in regard to baptism, namely that we teach through the Word that external baptism is a sign of the true baptism of Christ, that is of inner purification, rebirth and renewal; through which they should consider themselves and others honored and held in high esteem as those who are Christ's and will receive such an inner new birth; and that the cleansing from sin and the renewal of the disposition are due to Christ alone, who through His Spirit cleanses, gives faith and saves the elect. For this reason it is called *His* baptism, because He has earned and achieved such a Holy Spirit for us through His suffering.

131. The other reform or renewal in connection with baptism is that we have taught them neither to regard highly nor to use, chrism, oil salt bread and candles. The reason is that all these are little inventions of the human brain and have been accepted without any justification in the Word and have served to encourage much superstition. So it has become customary that such chrism and oil could be consecrated only by a bishop and only on a Maundy Thursday. Consequently many of the little children were not allowed to take a bath unless a parson had first released them for a penny or a *kreuzer*, that is, had washed of the chrism and the oil. Such hocus pocus ill becomes understanding, well informed Christians, who should highly regard and follow the Word of their Lord alone, and especially since there is no scriptural justification and it serves no good purpose, as has been evident in the past.

132. Therefore it is our custom to baptize our children without ostentation, after giving a short explanation of the significance and meaning of baptism, and having a common prayer that Christ should baptize the child through His Spirit and cleanse it from all sin, and then commending them to the godparents and the other brethren, that they should love them as members in Christ and as soon as possible lead them to Christ through proper instruction. For this we have nothing else but Scriptural justification. Since, then, the Scriptures teach all that is good, we consider it beneficial not to burden our members with any other ceremonies which would do our congregations no good at all but might even cause offense.

133. There are those,[50] however, who feel very strongly that we should have a third reform and change here, namely that we should not baptize the children at all; and feel that we have neither Scriptural Word nor example to do it. They claim that Christ commanded His disciples first to teach the nations and then to baptize them; similarly, the apostles baptized only those who had made a confession of their faith.

134. It is impossible to agree with them, and it does not follow, as they claim, that the apostles were sent by Christ to bring men to faith, and the beginning of that [faith] would have to be through teaching and preaching. Otherwise, who would wish to have himself or his children baptized? Without doubt, every apostle would have had to say with Paul: "Christ did not send me to baptize but to preach the Gospel" (1 Cor. 1:17). For this reason they prefer to deal primarily[51] with the adults; and, further, they prefer to describe how they dealt with the adults, since it was with them that their preaching was fruitful.

135. Nevertheless, as often as we read that the apostles baptized whole households, as Paul did in Corinth, the household of Stephana, in Philippi,

---

[50] the Anabaptists.
[51] *mit den verstendigen.*

the household of the seller of purple and the jail keeper (Acts 16:15, 33), and Peter, the household of Cornelius. It is quite obvious that not all of these had a true knowledge of the faith, for example the household of the jail keeper in Philippi, who listened to preaching for only half a night. For this reason we have demonstrated above that the baptism of John and the baptism of the apostles is one and the same. Now John baptized many who had very little knowledge of Christ; and even the apostles themselves, who baptized many other people (John 4:1–2), had a childlike faith. Yes, he and the apostles themselves many times even baptized those who had no faith at all, for example Simon the magician (Acts 8:13), with many others.

136. We are to pray for all men (1 Tim. 2:1), and since God does not regard the person, and since we in no way know whom God has chosen and whom He has rejected, it is our duty to regard everyone highly; and since baptism is an external thing, we should refuse no one whose godless life is not immediately known to us, whom we could no longer consider to be a little lamb. Therefore, since we do not know which children He has rejected, but do know that the children of the faithful are sanctified (1 Cor. 7:14), that is, they are now counted to be part of the household of God; moreover, since our Lord Jesus says that, to such belongs the Kingdom of God, and desired that they should be allowed to come to Him, embraced them and placed His hands upon them and blessed them (Mark 10:14–16), why then should we not baptize them, just as those in the Old Testament circumcised theirs? Especially since baptism is, for us, what circumcision was for the Jews.

137. Should you say, however, "But the Lord never baptized little children." Reply: you would find it difficult to show me an adult whom He baptized, for He Himself did not baptize anyone (John 4:2). And if you should find any justification in saying that the Lord said "of such" and not "of these" is the kingdom of heaven (Mark 10:14), as if he had meant, the kingdom of God belongs to those who humble themselves as children, for me it is enough that he embraced them and blessed them and says that whosoever receives a little child in His name receives Him, and he who does one of

them harm, for him it would be better to be drowned in the ocean; and their angels see the face of the Father (Mark 9:37, 42). All this indicates that little children are held in such high regard by God that they should be baptized, regardless of the fact that with some the water is wasted, as it was wasted on Simon the magician and many others.

138. In conclusion, no matter which way you turn or twist, you will have to grant me that baptism is an external matter which God did not limit to any time. For just as the Scriptures do not tie it down to any time, neither do they forbid it at any time. Therefore, then, it cannot be denied that it is a comfort to the parents that their children have been accepted by the congregation of Christ which prays for them, and that baptism given to children is the cause for parents and others to teach their children about Christ, to whom they have been dedicated in baptism, as soon as they are able to understand; therefore, it follows that it is far better to baptize children, and I will not say a word [to the effect] that it should be forbidden.

139. And should you quote many examples to show that it was customary to baptize those who already believed, I say that they baptized those too who did not believe, as I demonstrated above. In addition, there was no reason to write much about children, since the main purpose was to describe the fruits of the preaching of the apostles, and this would have been impossible in regard to infants, who couldn't speak. Yes, even if you should delay baptism for a long time, you will even so baptize many unbelievers, and by such delay you will deny the Christian life to many young people. Ah, they will say, but I am not yet a Christian; as soon as I become a Christian, then I will become devout.

140. Let us therefore, in complete trust and confidence, entrust our children to God. The Scriptures say many times that He carries the burdens of His own from Mother's womb, yes, even before they are born: why then should we regard them as unsanctified? Why make such a fuss over a lot of water? Since we are bidden to pray to God for all men: why should we then not

commend our little children to Him, especially since Christ showed such kindness to them? And even if we should baptize some billy-goats whom Christ would not have baptized through His Spirit, all that is involved is a lot of water and prayer. Even as far as the apostles were concerned, they did not always baptize those who believed.

141. It seems to me that the devil would like to divide us on account of external things, whom he is unable to divide on the main articles of the faith. Therefore, beloved brethren, who have the command of the Word, do not give the devil cause to celebrate. Always consider that the summary of the Law is to have love from a pure heart, a good conscience and a genuine faith, and do not be too much concerned about such external matters. Paul says that Christ had not sent him to baptize, but to preach the Gospel; therefore, wait patiently and desire earnestly that you should make known the baptism of Christ through the Holy Spirit, rather than that you should quarrel a great deal concerning baptism with water, and be confident that, just as the holy Fathers circumcised their children, we baptize ours in the assurance that they will be holy and children of God, and by so doing encourage one another to teach Christ to them more diligently, and to follow up such teaching more zealously as soon as they reach the age of understanding; and do not condemn us, you who in no wise can prove by Scripture that we are in error, nor that with such a baptism we act contrary to either faith or love. For we prove most diligently that baptism with water does not save, but only the spiritual baptism of Christ, which is its true meaning, and for which one should pray.

142. And would to God that you should admonish both yourselves and us with the same kind of concern regarding other matters which are far more important than this concern about baptism, and not undertake anything about which we do not have a Word of God or a Scriptural reference; then, to be sure, more patience, discipline and love would appear among us. Read the histories and the writings of the Fathers, and there you will find that from the very beginning of the Christian Church the enemy of unity

instigated, for the most part, all rifts and divisions through unnecessary battles over words or external things not essential for salvation. He is alert and stalks around like a roaring lion. Let us be brave and take good care to keep him from breaking in. Let us be diligent to study the teachings of Christ and of the apostles. How little you will find there concerning the Lord's Supper, how little concerning external baptism, but how much concerning the spiritual eating and drinking of the body and blood of Christ and concerning spiritual baptism, that is concerning faith, dying to sin, and a new spiritual life! Therefore, since we are to die to the worldly, external matters, let us then direct our thinking in all things to the spiritual, that is, to right faith and true love; let us treasure constantly in our hearts: "The Spirit gives life, the flesh is of no avail" (John 6:63), and further, let us never forget: "Knowledge puffs up, but love makes for growth; if someone, however, should think that he knows anything, he does not yet know what he should know. If someone, however, loves God, he will be known by Him" (1 Cor. 8:1–8).

143. Should there be, however, someone who delays baptism and desires to do so among those with whom he lives, without destroying love and unity, we in no way desire to quarrel with him about this, nor to condemn him. Everyone should be certain of his convictions. "The kingdom of God is not eating and drinking," neither is it baptism with water; "but righteousness, peace and joy in the Holy Spirit." He who serves Christ in this way "pleases God and is held in high esteem by men" (Rom. 14:17–18). Therefore I conclude here and now with the Apostle: "Let us strive after those things which serve for peace and for growth amongst us" (v. 19). So much on baptism.

X
Why We have Abolished Holy Days

144. Besides Sunday, there were many days ordained to be celebrated to the honor of God, His angels, and the departed saints, enforced by the ban and Christian obedience, that is, no work was to be done on these days and

whenever anyone did physical work out of necessity to some extent on those days, he was severely punished, yet it did not hinder him from eating to excess, drinking to excess, gambling and visiting prostitutes and everything else taught by the devil. In this way, the simple people were persuaded that to refrain from physical labor on those days was an exceptionally fine service to God, even though on those days most of the people served the devil partly through many superstitious actions such as masses, unintelligible songs, strange little prayers, buying indulgences and other things like that; and partly through all kinds of excesses and carnal pursuits, with which the riffraff offends God worse on these holy days than at any other time.

145. Paul writes: "Now that you have known God, or rather are known by God, how can you turn again to the weak and worthless ordinances which you desire to serve anew? You keep days and months and fasts and anniversaries: I fear for you lest I have worked for you in vain" (Gal. 4:9–11). Notice, then, the Apostle regards the keeping of days the equivalent of turning away from God and falling away from faith, that is why he is afraid that he has worked with them in vain, that is, that his preaching to them was done in vain. How many thousands there are now, who observe holy days as a necessary and meritorious service of God, which surely is nothing but a certain defection from faith! For Christ has set us free from the observance of all such external ordinances. He has set us free from all times, places, foods and whatever it may be, out of love and for the edification of our neighbor in order to serve in and with these things, and Paul states this quite clearly in all his epistles.

146. And since Paul earnestly dissuades them from such superstitious concern for days, where one day is held in higher regard than another, and where he speaks about this in the Scripture passage just quoted (*cf.* Col. 2:16), as well as in, it is fitting for us not to do less than this, since in our own time people show an even greater regard for these days. They believed that since God had commanded through Moses that some days should be

observed, it would be quite proper that they observe them, but their error was that they did not recognize that Christ had delivered them from those ordinances and that *He* is responsible for their salvation, not *they*, through such external ceremonies, since as yet they had not been thoroughly instructed in Christian freedom; but in our day they observe days which have been instituted merely by men and have adapted many pagan practices contrary to the clear command of God, with which they believe that they serve God in a special way when they practice some ostentatious church customs, and after that on those days much more than on any others delve themselves in all sort of evil and carnal practices; and it is not only God whom they think they serve in this way, but also the mother of Christ and the saints, and all sorts of innumerable errors are mixed in with it. And they cling a lot more obstinately to these errors than to the many divine and necessary commandments, disregarding the fact that Christ and the apostles have warned us diligently against such human teachings and commandments, and we realize quite clearly that the observance of holy days is the cause of and excuse for all sorts of evil practices. How, then, should a Christian, who should always be inclined and ready to advance the destruction of sin and the furtherance of righteousness, even at the cost of his life, have anything but disgust for these holy days and do everything in his power to abolish them?

147. And if someone should say, "Superstitions would be abolished if Christians would consider one day as another, and would in no way imply that the celebration was done either to influence God or to show respect to the saints in an anti-Christian way, and that on those days they would abolish all voluptuousness and carnal activities, and instead of that would listen to the Word of God and practice brotherly love." Reply: even if we were concerned to bring about all this through the Word alone without example, so that therefore all the abuses in connection with the holy days were abolished (this, of course, is impossible, since with deeds witness is borne to the words, and with Christ the Sabbaths are broken, and especially since those who allow themselves to be led by the Word are in the minority). Why,

then, should there be any reason to change the days, to establish useless celebrations, without a single Word of God? Should you point out those people for whom a favor is being done in this way: "know, then, that we should win people's favor only by doing good things" (Rom. 15:2), so that it may serve them for growth. He who would please people in other ways should not aspire to be a servant of Christ, as Paul writes when he speaks about the observance of such external ceremonies which many people often had observed to their own harm.

148. Therefore, if in a certain place the Gospel is being preached for the first time, and holy days are allowed until the Gospel has been preached for some time, so that the people are not frightened away from the Word through an untimely abolition until they become more thoroughly acquainted with it, then a real service will be done for the people and a favor will be done them for their advancement. We have discussed this at length above. When, however, the Gospel has been preached for some time and often, and it is quite clearly understood that one day should be regarded like any other day; whoever would then allow the observance of holy days for the sake of pleasing people by doing wrong, would do them wrong, for he would encourage them in the superstitions of the times, or a high regard for the enemies of God and enjoy their favor, but would fear them more than God.

149. For how could anyone who does not have extra food, but would like very much to feed his wife and child, observe so many holy days, if he knew for certain that neither God nor the saints are pleased thereby, and that he would not frighten off a few nasty people, to whom Christian freedom is abhorrent, by using them (the days, to earn money for food)? Regardless of which of these two is the reason, neither should count, and such weaker brethren should also be strengthened with examples of Christian freedom.

150. And there are others who want to enhance the malicious twist of their unbelieving hearts by saying: all external things are indifferent, why should I not then either celebrate or work, just as it suits me? When indeed it is neither superstition nor un-Christian timidity toward evil people which makes them observe the holy days. They should consider that Paul says: "I have indeed the authority to do all things, but not all things are useful; I have all authority, but not all things edify. Let no one seek his own good, but let everyone seek that of his neighbor" (1 Cor. 10:23–24). So then, as far as you are concerned, you are free to celebrate or not to celebrate; but since you should not live for yourselves but for your neighbor, and should undertake nothing which does not help the other, how will you then observe those holy days which have been instituted contrary to the Word of God and consequently are not edifying in any way? For all those things which are good and edifying have been clearly and abundantly declared in the Scriptures.

151. But why should we waste any more words? It is quite clear that among all the ordinances of men, observance of the holy days has been the most harmful; for not only have they in themselves been harmful to faith and love, so that many foolish people believed that with their idleness they were doing great service to God and His saints, when instead on those days they should and ought to do good deeds for their neighbor, just as the Lord taught it with words and deeds. For the Sabbath is, as God commanded, made for the sake of men, when good deeds should be done for the neighbor, but I would rather keep silent concerning our holy days, which have not been commanded by God and which therefore no one can force us to keep (Col. 2:16). According to their opinion, they cannot do it since it is a mortal sin, but instead they have promoted and strengthened all sorts of errors, superstitions, blasphemies of God, as well as all kinds of carnal sins and immoralities. When did the false prophets mislead the people more than on holy days? When did the priests benefit more from their blasphemies and pretentious Masses than on holy days? When was the sale of in-

dulgences, howling and bawling [in the churches][52] held in higher regard than on holy days? When was the worship of the saints and all kinds of superstition practiced more than on holy days, and since I am speaking of physical vices, when do you find more pride, ostentation, excessive eating, excessive drinking, impurity and murder of souls than on holy days? It is quite clear and cannot be denied that the holy days destroy everything that is good and initiate everything that is evil; and everyone can see quite clearly that these evil, poisonous fruits are the result of the planting, not of the Father but of the enemy of all good things, the devil.

152. Since God has commanded us to root out all such practices, we have put forth every effort to the end that Christians should consider one day as good as another; and that we should worship God every single day, that is, let Him work and create, and that they should submit themselves gladly to His will. And even though some have said for quite some time that the abuses should be abolished with the Word, and that the holy days should be retained, it has been our experience, and it is so required by the Scriptures, that one should bear witness to one's beliefs with deeds. Paul, when he speaks about holy days, says: "Be like me, for I am like you" (Gal. 4:12), that is, to you who are without the Law I have become as one without the Law, but now be also as I am, free Christians who put their whole trust in Christ alone and not in external matters. Therefore, since we must preach that one day is as good as another, why should we ourselves act differently? We must teach that we should think every day of Christ's birth, circumcision, death, suffering and resurrection, and be thankful to God for them every day, and should we then choose special days for this purpose? If we did, we would be responsible for the hypocrisy of many who are not necessarily the worst people, even if their attitudes were to remain unchanged; by doing so, God would be angered and insulted all the more, and we would encourage and sustain the regard for the distinction between the days.

---

[52] In D. S. but not in Walch.

153. In addition, if we should be without any Word of God for some things, what then would be the outcome in regard to them? Wise is he who benefits from the harmful experiences of others: and we have no inclination to be made wise through our own. We cannot deny that the old fathers were ill advised when they retained a few holy days for the sake of those who loved the world too much, hoping that they would hear some portion of the Word of God. And we experience daily how dreadfully the devil harms the godliness and honor of many because of the holy days, and we are satisfied with ourselves and must admit that we keep some holy days for the benefit of the servants or whoever else might benefit by them.

154. However, should someone say, "Abolish Sundays as well." Reply: this does not follow. We are told in the Ten Commandments to celebrate the seventh day, so that the laborers and the servants should have their day of rest (Exod. 20:8–11; Deut. 5:12–15). Love cannot allow us to restrict such rest. Therefore on six days we should work, as it is expressed in the Lord's commands, and rest on the seventh. Since, then, a Christian will always prefer to observe ordinances which are not contrary to God rather than to make ordinances himself, and just as he should always be more eager to serve than to be served, there is therefore no reason why Sunday, which has been observed for many generations by Christians everywhere as the seventh day, should be abolished. If we should celebrate one day out of seven, as love requires, then Sunday is just as good as any other day; and since on that day we rest physically, it is quite proper that the Christian congregation should assemble, listen to the Word of God, pray and observe the Lord's Supper. And therefore Sunday is not a special feast day, and no superstitious service of worship is held as on the other holy days. Since, however, the observance of Sunday has also been so abominably misused, such abuses should be abolished by the faithful through the Word of God, and through the wise ordering by the Christian authorities [over] the rest of the people; and this would be easier to accomplish on the one and only Sunday than on so many holy days.

155. It is quite obvious, then, that brotherly love requires the celebration of Sunday, but not all of the other holidays; on the contrary, since they are harmful to the neighbor, as we have shown, they should not be allowed at all. This is our justification[53] for abolishing them, but for retaining the celebration of Sunday, and for abolishing with all diligence those abuses which have crept in. But in such a way that love, which requires the observance of Sunday, should be lord, to direct and maintain the same in the best way which is helpful to the neighbor and that it should always be manifest that the Sabbath has been established for the sake of man, and not man for the sake of the Sabbath, who, along with Christ, should be the lord of the Sabbath, and should, if he is to be of any use at all to any one, know how to use Christian freedom, not like the Jews and their descendants, the Papists, who claim that if it should happen that anything useful was done for the neighbor on Sunday, the observance would be broken.

156. Now if someone should say: "In the Law there were many holidays, such as the first and the last of seven days at Easter, on which unleavened bread had to be eaten; the day of firstlings; the first and tenth days of the seventh month, and seven whole days at the celebration of the Feast of the Tabernacles, during which they were supposed to rest and remember the divine blessings with thanksgiving: is it not possible, then, that in addition to Sunday, the free love of God and of the neighbor should call for the celebration of Christmas, the Circumcision of the Lord, the Three Kings' Day and Ascension?"

157. Reply: the divine blessings which are supposed to be recalled on such days should be recalled by the Christian daily, and he should never set a special time for such remembrances without Scriptural authority; otherwise the simple people will again be led to hold in high regard the shadows, pictures, paltry ordinances concerning external things, and will become accustomed to regard one day more highly than another; love, of course, which is

---

[53] *ursach*

ineffective unless it serves to bring about change for the better, cannot allow this. But nothing which is undertaken without the authority of the Word of God will bring about this improvement. The Law does not state that Moses instituted those holy days just mentioned, other than the seventh day, in order to give rest to the animals, the servants and employees, so neither does love require us Christians to observe the same holy days.

158. Therefore, if in the daily preaching the masters should be reminded to give their servants what is their due, and remind them that they, too, have a Lord, it will follow logically that the servants will have as many days to celebrate as those under the Law. Many of the trades allow a half day off once a week as a holiday: and since among us all the servants are free, they can, if they so desire, require as many holidays from their masters as they please, so that love certainly does not require any other holidays; and even those holidays just mentioned, such as Christmas, New Year's Day and others, should not be tolerated. For through such celebration the error that one day is better than another would be maintained; and besides this, there is not a single feast which has not attached to it its own superstition and excesses.

159. For example, when the alarm bell is rung at Christmas, water is supposed to turn into wine, they eat excessively and drink excessively after the three required Masses, and observe the holy days with pomp and excesses. On the Day of Circumcision, following pagan practices, the good year is celebrated with much superstition. On the Three Kings' Day, kings are crowned and the Saturnalia is celebrated. On Ascension Day lambs are cut into little pieces. And who wants to list all the superstitions and pagan abuses observed according to the custom of each place? Therefore love requires that they should be abolished.

160. Should you say, "These abuses ought to be abolished through the Word." Reply: not all accept the Word, but it is necessary for the great majority of people, if the abuses of those days mentioned are to be abolished, that certainly the days themselves should be abolished. Besides, among

those who accept them there are many weak people who require an example which should eradicate among them the superstitions connected with those days. Thus, since the faithful do not need any set days to remind themselves of the divine mercies, and since we cannot deny that such days are harmful to the great mass of people who must be ruled through law and order, and who know nothing better than to use freedom from physical labor for voluptuous idleness: why then should we not abolish every single one of those holy days which have no Scriptural foundation and which have brought the Word much hindrance and have done great harm to all decency and whose observance by the minority cannot be defended? We preach here twice every day, often three times; would to God the concern were so great that we would have cause to preach more often; that task would be no burden to us. In addition we admonish employers to be kind to their servants and to encourage them in all godly things, which might be better accomplished through the Word than through the observance of the holy days by the servants, the young and the great mass of people.

161. Since we have no reason to retain one feast and reject another, and since it cannot be denied that all have been harmful and the great ones most of all, we shall be satisfied with the observance of Sunday alone, which is the only one required by brotherly love. And God grant us grace that through the Word we will be enabled to get rid of the abuses, even here where they have been the least. And further, we have no doubt our office requires the abolition of all other holy days, because it is pleasing to God and will be highly advantageous to the congregation of God and will serve to their edification. In regard to sermons, which some claim to be the cause of disputes and which are not very highly esteemed by them, they will not be restricted in any way. And those who are not misled because of their love of quarreling or their superstitious regard for the days, will admit and accept this too. Everyone look to himself; our heart is not just, merely because we think that it is just; all the malice of the heart is known to God alone.

XI
The Reason Why Images Should Be Abolished

162. We have also preached against idols and images. The honorable Council has made a survey, and all images in the foremost churches which have been especially esteemed have been removed. The Christian congregation which I serve has removed all images and pictures out of its church; for they were unanimous and have not been hindered, as has been the case in some other churches or congregations, by the bishopric or some other opposing authority. The leaders of the congregation of God in Zurich have given more than sufficient, clear, Scriptural proof that it is Christian and justified, and would be even more Christian to remove all idols and images quietly and without fuss from all churches; there is no reason why we should say any more about this here.

163. The first commandment of God, of the ten, is plain enough, where He commands: "I am the Lord, your God, who has led you out of the land of Egypt, out of the house of bondage. You are to have no other gods beside me. You are to make no image or any kind of likeness of anything, either of that which is in heaven above, nor that which is on the earth, nor that which is in the water below the earth; do not worship them and do not serve them" (Exod. 20:2–5). In these words, which contain the basic principle[54] which can be found here and there in the Law and the Prophets against idols and images, everyone who seeks truth will understand that God has forbidden the making of idols and images; and further that no one should honor them, esteem or serve them, for by so doing the one true God is insulted and slighted.

164. For in itself an idol is nothing, or nothing more than an artifact made by human hands, just like any other thing made through skills given by God. For this reason, therefore, they may be retained, provided there is true

---
[54] *grund*

faith; just as Solomon used lion idols on the steps approaching his throne, idols of cows on which the molten sea rested and many other things, roses and the like.

165. Therefore in all places where idols and images are forbidden, it is found that the reason why they are forbidden was that no one should do honor to them nor serve God through them, since by doing so the heart is estranged from true faith and attaches itself to external things. That is the abomination before God; and this is the reason why idols and images are forbidden everywhere in the Scriptures and threatened against. Now no one can deny that the idols and images in our churches were made in order to please God; they are worshipped, that is people bow down before them, uncover their heads and genuflect before them, and the little Hebrew word, translated, "to worship," means that. Vows are made to them, pilgrimages are made to them, sacrifices are offered to them, they are beautifully decorated and ornamented, special buildings and enclosures are built for them. And what more should we say? Whatever practices were customary before idolatrous images, are also observed before these. For this reason, for many people they are no longer simply idols, but most abominable idols which harm the poor people, and harm their faith and love even more.

166. Therefore all Christians should spare no effort to abolish them; first of all through the Word in their hearts, and after that in deed with the eyes, for the sake of the weak and the simple, who, regardless of how vehemently opinions are expressed in speech and sermon, still retain the superstitious awe of the idols. We have preached with all diligence for a long time here that God should be worshipped in spirit and not through idols; money should be spent and good deeds done, not to dumb images made by hands, but to the living images of God, our neighbors. Further, since by order of our honorable Council [only] the worst idols, to whom the foolish people have burnt the most candles and which they worshipped the most, have been abolished, there were not a few who at one time believed that they thoroughly understood the Word, but complained vociferously against such

abolition of images, but who now, through such action and the influence of the Word, have entirely rejected the idols and the images. So deeply had this superstition and regard of images been rooted, that many needed to have the Word reinforced by active example. It is up to the authorities to abolish a public offense when there is no willing cooperation on the part of the congregation, and not to any one person, just as we read that neither prophets nor apostles, much as they preached and wrote against idolatry, took active part in the abolition of a single idol themselves. At the time of Isaiah, Jeremiah and all the Prophets, there were many idols in Jerusalem, and even though they preached against them with zeal, they did not remove a single one by their own hand.

168. For he who is not set over other people should teach only with words, and should bear witness by his own example; any further action is not proper, except only by those who have been set over others. Therefore, just as John preached freely to Herod that he should not have Herodias, the wife of his brother Philip, he still did not, along with his followers, take her away from him and stone her according to the prescription of the Law concerning the punishment of adulteresses. Why? He had no command, and therefore did not carry the sword. Consequently, should you see someone kneel before an image and venerate it, according to the Law, he should die; but just as little as you would presume to execute this judgment, since you do not carry the sword nor are set in a position of authority, just so little should you presume to remove and destroy his idol.

169. And should you quote Moses to me, who without any special command killed the Egyptian who killed a Hebrew; or Pineas, the son of Eleazar, who stabbed to death Simri, a captain of the Simeonites who whored with a prostitute, or even Elijah, who strangled those who sacrificed to Baal, I reply: examine the Scriptures concerning all three, and you will find that none of them did this without express command. Moses had already been appointed by God to be the judge and avenger of the Israelites, as is stated by Stephen (Acts 7:22–25). Similarly, before Pineas executed

his deed, God commanded that everyone should strangle his captains if they became involved with prostitutes (Num. 25:4–5). And again, Elijah had the consent of all the people, who themselves apprehended those who sacrificed to Baal (1 Kings 18:40).

170. But surely, if the authorities desire to be Christian and to follow the example of the devout Josiah, they should first proclaim the Law of God to the people, and should again establish the divine covenant with them: therefore it is up to them to abolish energetically all such abominations related to idols and images, even though many who are displeased with such actions remain in the congregation. They are required at all times to be the official representatives of God and should govern in such a way that the people would follow God, who is the true Overlord, and in this follow the example of David (Ps. 7:8–9). Therefore, it is impossible to deny that the idols harm both faith and love; faith, since more is expected from one image than another, in receiving mercy and help, and further because they believe it to be pleasing to God to make idols and decorate and venerate them; love, because so much money is spent on them which should have been spent on the poor, and further because the idols are used as decoys, so that even more is given to the useless, shorn knaves; I will not say another word concerning the great superstition, the magic and the deceiving sleights-of-hand, countless in number, which are seen here and there, but particularly in connection with pilgrimages. And it surely follows that the Christian authorities should abolish such offenses and hindrances to the Kingdom of God, for in connection with evil deeds they are to be feared.

171. And should this not please everyone, let them consider that, if they promote that which is Christian and honorable, it probably will not in any way please the great masses who are good for nothing anyway. The authorities are servants of the law, which in no way releases the unrighteous, the disobedient, the profane, etc.; "for the righteous man no law has been given" (1 Tim. 1:9). And wherever there are Christian congregations, they should zealously plead and appeal to the authorities to abolish the idols and

everything else which is contrary to all salutary teaching, since there are many who are weak and who need a true, active example of the Word. For even though everyone should know that an idol is nothing and no one should take offense, this unfortunately is not so, and is evident daily: also, since we have only one God, who is invisible and whom no man has seen at any time, and only one Christ, who indeed was a man but whose human and physical presence cannot be seen by the eyes, since this would be of no value to us anyway; similarly we, too, should worship God in spirit and in truth, and spend our money on the poor and do them good as the Lord says: "Sell all you have and give it to the poor" (Matt. 19:21), and should it not be an abomination to us to allow so many idols and images in our churches, contrary to the Word of God, which find their source in many idolatrous fables, when instead we should teach and obey the Word of God alone?

172. It is true, the idols must first of all be torn out of the hearts, and that by means of the Word, and then they can harm no one. But to be sure, whoever has torn them out of his heart will dislike being surrounded by them, since he knows that divine honor is shown to them and will continue to be shown to them by many others. And if they were of such little harm, why then did God, who always is the wisest, and commands and forbids nothing in vain, so insistently forbid them everywhere in the Scriptures? Should you say, "we are free of the Law." Reply: yes, the little group of the elect; the others, the large masses, require today, as much as at the time of Moses, to be governed by law and the sword; and therefore those commands which are concerned with faith and love, like the Ten Commandments in which idols are forbidden in the first one, should be practiced and obeyed by everyone everywhere.

173. And what is the good of all the images, since from time immemorial they have been the cause of great offense and harm, like all things which are undertaken contrary to the Word of God? For this reason, he who is a Christian and knows that all things should serve for growth, and that things

which are offensive should be abolished, will recognize that it is highly useful and salutary to abolish idols and images everywhere. God grant that this may be accomplished. The lay people should be taught with the Word of God and not with dumb blocks, stones and paintings, for little was accomplished by the Fathers through idolatrous practices. It is a fleshly, fleeting devotion which is furthered through nothing more than the beholding of images. If you are a Christian, then listen to this: the Word is sufficient to inspire you to do all that which is good.

174. And I want to explain one more thing: in the church, Saint Aurelian by name, where I am a servant of the Word, we have had our special idol, a coffin and a tomb in which St. Aurelia, one of the 11,000 young women who died of the fever when that same group passed by Strasbourg, and who allegedly was buried in the grave just mentioned, and to whose sanctity two miracles were ascribed. The one: that at one time some soldiers, looking for treasures in her coffin, were made insane by St. Aurelia for such desecration, and that she herself chewed of their fingers and their hands, and all of them died. The other: there were some who dug for lime on her day, and since they did not pay proper respect to the day dedicated to her, were killed by the vengeful maiden. For 1100 years she is supposed to have remained in her grave; but it was only during the last 100 years that her grave was elevated, since it was hoped that it would be profitable. It is only very recently that people have thronged to it. Many pilgrimages were made to the grave, most of them on account of the fever. People ate the soil around it; a small idol stood on the altar, and it was decorated and ornamented, and shirts were hung around the grave to serve as lures.

175. All this is contrary to faith and love. And therefore, after sufficient instruction in the Word of God, the minister of the congregation did away with that same tomb; and the bones which were found were very large and irregular, so that it would have been impossible for them to have come from one body, namely that of a young girl, and were removed from the sight of the people. It is God who should be worshipped in all places with faith, and

not the dead saints; for those practices there is no Word of God, and there is no one who is more inclined to be merciful and to help us than our God and Father. Now, through the prominence given to this tomb, many people came from afar to seek its help and to find God by the grave, and instead of helping the poor, their gifts were given to wooden idols and bones.

176. First of all the shirts and other lures were removed, and after that the small idol. The vault which contained the tomb was kept closed, in order to turn people away from such an offense. Nothing was of any use: they preferred to push their shirts and other superstitious gifts through the lattice work, rather than to give them to the naked Christ as He is revealed in so many poor children and others. The congregation of Christ, in order to prevent the search for a strange God among them, removed the tomb entirely and covered up the vault; since they as Christians did not want to suffer the existence of such a delusion, which had become so offensive.

177. And no one should counter that holy bones were held in high regard at the time of the Fathers, or that great miracles were done by their graves. The Fathers, too, could have been mistaken; just as, even at the time of the Apostles, many errors crept in, according to the writings of the Apostles. So it was the custom among the Fathers to venerate the graves of the martyrs for this reason alone, that through their steadfastness others would be encouraged to like steadfastness in their faith, and not because they desired to seek special help. Soon the devil got mixed up in all this with counterfeit miracles (*cf.* Matt. 24:24); many foolish people sought their help and comfort, which should come from the one true God alone, at the graves of the dead, and left many contributions at such places in order to be set free; it is a well-known fact that prostitutes and knaves carry away the best booty, with the exception of those which have been placed or hung on stone, iron and wood, or have been burned in oil and wax.

178. Therefore, to be sure, he who loves Christ will help and advise that such idolatry and superstition and harmful abuses, which arose and were

practiced contrary to the Word of God, should be abolished. True miracles happen as a confirmation of the Word of God and for the establishment of the sole honor of God (Mark 6), and in many other passages of Scripture, and not to confirm such idolatrous superstition, and not to seek the mercy of God and His help in one place more than another, for the sake of a little basket full of bones; bones are bones, they are not God.

XII
Why Songs and Prayers in the Church Have Been Changed

179. It has been customary, and continues to be so, that many prescribed songs and prayers are used in the Masses and at the Divine Offices[55] for payment of money, and this is done by those who do not yet know Christ, and is done in many places contrary to the Scriptures, and drawn out of fables, such as: collects and prayers of St. Barbara, St. Catherine, St. Christopher, St. Margaret, St. George and many more; in addition they sing and read such prayers and songs in Latin, which the ordinary man cannot understand at all, and they themselves often hardly understand. Furthermore, they have attached these to times, places and numbers, contrary to the fashion of prayer and divine praise, which should be spontaneous.

180. Now, since we know that only the Spirit of God can know divine things (1 Cor. 2:10–11), and further that the Scriptures of God contain nothing but good (2 Tim. 3:16), therefore in the congregation of God we use neither songs nor prayers which are not based on Holy Scripture. And since all the actions of the congregation of God should serve for the edification of every man, we pray and sing nothing except in the common German language, so that the lay people are able to say "amen" together as it is taught by the Spirit of God (1 Cor. 14:16).

181. To the Latin language, which does not contain anything that is good or useful which could not be said more artistically and better in the Hebrew

---

[55] *Siebenzeiten* - the customary monastic seven daily services.

and Greek languages, regardless of whether it deals with divine or natural matters; and which was used by the old Romans and even more so by the new Papists to blind other nations and to bring them into subservience and to [hem them in] in this manner, because it has been most profitable to them, we will not give the honor of holding back the congregation of God by first translating that which is helpful for the lay people to know.

182. Further, since it is an insult to God not to pray and sing from the heart, we have decided not to attach these to any special time in the congregation nor to circumscribe them with all sorts of conditions but voluntarily, on Sundays, when the Lord's Supper is observed, we pray and sing briefly. Everything is based on the Scriptures, this and the reasons for it have been explained above. Similarly at vespers, since the physical celebration should be used for growth of the spirit, we sing one, two or three psalms with a prophecy, that is, an exposition of a chapter or so of Holy Scripture; and in the same way also, daily the whole congregation sings a psalm before and after the sermon.

183. And furthermore, no services are held for the assembled congregation without sermons, but the spirit and devotion of each one is encouraged, to pray and to praise God without ceasing, by himself in his heart, so that we may not be tempted, contrary to the teachings of Jesus, to make many words in our prayers (Matt. 6:7), or to insult God with pretense and hypocrisy, more than to praise Him, and this would happen if it were not done from the heart.

184. And in this we know with certainty that we are obeying the teaching of the Spirit of God (1 Cor. 14:1–40, etc.). Paul writes: "Let the Word of God dwell in you richly in all wisdom, teach and exhort one another with psalms and songs of praise and spiritual songs" (Col. 3:16), in the mercy of God, "and sing to the Lord in your hearts" In the same manner he wrote also to the Ephesians that we should love God with all our might, why should we then not sing to Him also, as did the saints of the Old and New Testa-

ments? As long as such singing is done from the heart, not with the mouth alone, but that it should spring forth and come out of the heart; and this is what the Apostle means when he says: "and sing to the Lord from your hearts." For his meaning is not that we should sing without a voice, for then it would be impossible for us to encourage and edify the others, or how else could we speak with one another, concerning that which he writes to the Ephesians?

185. Therefore, those who discard singing in the congregation of God know little, either about the contents of Scripture or the custom of the first apostolic churches and congregations, who always praised God with singing. For that purpose the Psalms were mostly used; and this we read not only in the writings of Paul and our historians, but also in the writings of the pagans, for example Pliny II. And Christ Himself concluded His Last Supper and last sermon with a song of praise (Matt. 26:30). There are, however, some people who have such a love which cannot be pleased with anything unless they initiate it. For this reason, therefore, we have given the fundamental reasons[56] why we have changed prayers and songs, and the righteous certainly could not be displeased with this. May God help the others that He Himself and His Word may please them, and so we surely will be able to get along well with one another.

186. We have also undertaken changes in other matters, namely, that nowadays there is no longer a candle burned in the congregation, no holy salt or holy water are used, after a funeral the dead are commended to God, since the spirits of all the faithful are in His hands. The reason for such and other reforms has been publicized quite often; the Scriptures, which teach only that which is good, teach nothing about such things; and in addition they have been used to the harm of faith and love, therefore Christians should tread carefully concerning them.

---

[56] *Grund und Ursach*

187. Therefore we ask all those who love the Gospels that they should regard with faithful and simple eyes all the reasons just listed, for the changes which have been made among us, according to the Scriptures of God, and should make use of Christian freedom in external things in such a way that their first concern should always be those things which are edifying and useful; and further to take to heart that even though the idols are nothing, all external ceremonies are free in themselves, yet there are very few who will recognize these things as nothing and free in truth, even though they may have said so for a long time. For to be sure, whenever these are recognized as nothing and especially since they have done much harm in the past, and even at the present time are a stumbling block to many weak brethren, one should not worry too much about these things, yes, it would be far better to bear witness to such insight with a deed for the strengthening of others.

188. There are some who believe that we should go slowly in these matters for the sake of Christian freedom, when to be sure we are hindered by the fleshly freedom, which is afraid of the cross and in this way opposes the godless and deals with the weaklings somewhat more firmly. How often does it happen that we give as an excuse the weakness of the people, when in reality it is our own weakness that holds them back? Nothing should be attempted with tumult and noise—therefore he who does not first preach diligently, and desires to attack something before the faithful are in full agreement, him we will in no wise accept as one of us; neither [will we accept] those who do not primarily preach about faith and love. On the other hand, we cannot praise those who disregard external things to such an extent that they not only fail to avoid the idols and ceremonies which they can see, unless they are completely blind, to be not only nothing, but actually very harmful to many simple people, but even close their eyes to the luxury of clothing, cowardly and excessive carousing, and even worse things than these. The Lord grant that His Word may be preached everywhere in single-minded sincerity, which Word, to be sure, is mighty enough in itself to abolish, without noise and in a salutary manner, everything which finds no jus-

tification in it and which therefore is no good, and no one should undertake anything, no matter how free it may be in itself, unless it serves for edification. For we should always live for others and not for ourselves. And furthermore [God grant] that we who have been inspired by one and the same spirit in all things external and internal, may be one in thought, word and deed, according to the Word of God, then Christian freedom will not be harmed, no human ordinances will be established, but we will live according to the divine commandments, to the praise of God and to the eternal salvation of our neighbor. God grant this. Amen.

189. The contents of this little book are the common faith of those of us who are in the ministry and under compulsion to preach the Gospel publicly here in Strasbourg, we who, according to all divine Scriptures, direct all our preaching to this end, that faith in God and love to the neighbor, which are the sources of true morality and constant patience, should always be planted, increased and strengthened in our listeners, and that everyone should use external ceremonies such as the Lord's Supper, Baptism, and others, for the growth of faith and love, as has been set forth in this little book. And therefore, if anyone should teach or print anything which is contrary to the content of this book and should claim to find its origin here [in Strasbourg], it should not be ascribed to us, for it has been done without our knowledge and consent, and therefore we will not be held responsible for it. However, as to that which is set forth and is taught in this and other writings sent out by us, we offer to give to all who desire it, sufficient reasons and justification[57] based on Holy Scriptures; and our names are:

Wolfgangus Capito	Antonius Firn
Caspar Hedio	Martinus Hag
Mattheus Zell	Martinus Butzer
Symphorian Pollio	
Theobaldus Niger	

---

[57] *Grund und Ursach*

Author's Bibliography

Thompson, Bard "Liturgies of the Western Church", Cleveland, N.Y., 1961 References to *Martini Buceri Opera Omnia. Series I. Deutsche Schriften,* Vol. I, 1960; Vol. II, 1962 (edited by Robert Stupperich), indicated as either *Deutsche Schriften I* or *Deutsche Schriften II*; and references to J. Georg Walch, "Doktor Martin Luthers Sämmtlichte Schriften" (Neue revidierte Stereotypausgabe), St. Louis, Mo., 1904; indicated as *Walch*.

Bucer's Works

June 17-20, 1523. Mart. Buceri Verantwortung ahn M. h. uff Episcopi Schriben seiner persohn halben ahm ein Rath 1523. *Deutsche Schriften I:293-301.*

August 1523. Das ym selbs niemant, sonder anderen leben soll, und wie der mensch dahin Kummen mog. Martinus Butzer. *Deutsche Schriften I:44-67*

August 1523. Martin Butzers an ein christlichen Rath und Gemyn der Statt Weissenburg Summary seiner Predig daselbst gethon. *Deutsche Schriften I:79-147.*

Oct./Nov. 1523. Das D. Luthers vnd seiner nachfolger lehre, wie die inn iren buchern verfasset ist, in den Hauptarticulen vnd puncten christlich vnd gerecht ist. Vnnd nit ein newe, sonder die alte vnd ewige lehre ist vnd bleiben wird. *Deutsche Schriften I:310-344.*

Fall 1523. Verantwortung M. Butzers. Uff das im seine widerwertigen, ein theil mit der worheit, ein theil mit lugen, zum argsten zumessen. *Deutsche Schriften I:156-184.*

October 20, 1524. Ein kurzer wahrhafftiger bericht von Disputationem und gantzen handel, so zwischen Cunrat Treger, Provincial der Augustiner, und den predigern des Evangelii zu Strassburg sich begeben hat. *Deutsche Schriften II:37-173.*

Dec. 26, 1524. Grund und Ursach ausz gotlicher schrifft der neuwerungen an dem nachtmal des herren, so man die Mess nennet, Tauff, Feyrtagen, bildern und gesang in der gemein Christi, wann die zusamenkompt, durch und auf das wort gottes zu Straszburg furgenomen *Deutsche Schriften I:194-278 Walch XX:352-439.*

January 1526. Psalter wol verteutscht ausz der heyligen sprach. *Deutsche Schriften II:187-222.*

May 1526. Rathschleg M. butzers vom singen, lesen, vszlegen und tisch des herren *Deutsche Schriften II:470-482.*

March 29, 1527. Praefatio M. Buceri in quartum tomum Postilae Lutheranae *Walch XVII:1584-1605.*

Spring 1527. Das Martin Butzer Sich in verteutschung des Psalters Johann Pommers getrewlich und Christlich gehalten . . . . hat *Deutsche Schriften II:265-275.*

January 22, 1528. Martin Butzers Predig gethon zu Bern Von der nachvolgung Christi *Deutsche Schriften II:281-294.*

June 21, 1528. Vergleichung D. Luthers und seins gegentheyls vom Abentmal Christi. Dialogus. Das ist eyn freündlich desprech. *Deutsche Schriften: II:305-383.*

October 12, 1528. (Buceri Bedencken) Das die Messz die schwerist gottisschmach vnd abgottery vnd von keiner christlichen oberkeitt zu dulden sey *Deutsche Schriften: II:532-537.*

June 1531. Christlich Leeren, Ceremonien vnnd leben *Deutsche Schriften: II:417-419*

Luther's Works

Kritische Gesamtausgabe der Werke D. Luthers, Weimar, 1883ff (W. A.).

Kritische Gesamtausgabe (Briefwechsel), Weimar (W.A., Br.).

1519. Sermon vom Sacrament des heiligen Leichnams Christi W.A., II, 743ff.

August 3, 1520. Sermon von dem neuen Testament, das ist von der heiligen

Messe W. A., VI, 363ff.

1520. Von der Babylonischen Gefangenschaft der Kirche Walch XIX:4-129.

1520. De Captivitate Babylonica ecclesiae praeludium W. A., VI, 497ff.

1520. Von der Freiheit eines Christenmenschen W. A. VII, 20ff.

December 1523. Vom Anbeten des heiligen Leichnams Christi W. A. XI, 431 ff.

1525. Wider die himmlischen Propheten W. A. XVIII, 203.

1528. Vom Abendmahl Christi, Bekenntnis. W. A. XXVI, 261 ff.

September 1544. D. Martin Luthers Kurzes Bekenntnis vom heiligen Sacrament wider die Schwärmer. W. A. LVI, 41ff.

Carlstadt's Works

June 24, 1521. Von den Empfahern, Zeichen und Zusage des heiligen Sacraments des Fleisches und Blutes Christi Walch XX:2288-2307.

March 1524. Von den zweyen Hochsten gebotten der lieb Erich Hertzsch: *Karlstadts Schriften aus den Jahren 1523-25*, Teil I, Nr. III.

Oct.–Nov. 1524. Dialogus oder ein gesprechbuchlin Von dem grewlichen vnnd abgottischen miszbrauch des hochwirdigsten sacraments Jesu Christi. Walch XX: 2312-2359; Hertzsch, *op. cit.* Nr. V.

September 1524. Wider die alten und neuen papistischen Messen Walch XX: 23-6-2313.

November 1524. Ob man gemach faren vnd des egernussen der schwachen verschonen soll in sachen so gottis willen angehn Hertzsch, *op. cit.*, Nr. IV.

November 1524. "Vrsachen der halben Andres Carolstadt ausz den landen zu Sachsen vertryben" Hertzsch, *op. cit.*, B Nr. Vi.

Other Primary Sources

Bucer, Martin. "Miscellaneous Liturgical Writings", photographically reproduced MSS from Thomasstift, Strassburg. In U. T. S. Library.

April 30, 1518. List of books in Bucer's Library *Deutsche Schriften I:281-284.*
April 29, 1521. Bucer's dismissal from the Dominican order. *Deutsche Schriften I:285-290.*

Mid-November 1523. Bucer's request for citizenship in Strassburg. *Deutsche Schriften I:302-303.*

March 29, 1523. The congregation of St. Aurelia requests the Rath that Bucer's election as their pastor be ratified. *Deutsche Schriften I:366-368.*

1524-1531. Proposals of the Strassburger preachers in regard to the educational system, to the Rat. *Deutsche Schriften II:387-422.*

1525-1529. Proposals by the Strassburg preachers to the Rat in regard to the abolition of the Mass and reorganization of the ecclesiastical life. *Deutsche Schriften II:423-545*

Enders, Ludwig. "Aus dem Kampf der Schwärmer gegen Luther." Drei Flugschriften aus den Jahren 1524, 1525 Halle A. S., 1893.

Letters

(1) Bonnet, Jules. "Letters of John Calvin." Philadelphia, 1858.

(2) Individual Letters:

Capito. "Was man halten und antworten soll von der Spaltung zwischen." Martin Luther und Andreas Carlstadt.

September 18, 1524. Luther to Gerbel. W. A., Br. III, 352.

November 16, 1524. Zwingli to Matthaeus Alber. Walch XVII:1512-1529.

November 22, 1524. Gerbel to Luther. W. A., Br. III, 378-380.

November 23, 1524. The Strassburg preachers to Luther. W. A., Br. III, 381-

387.

December 14, 1524. Luther to Spalatin. W. A., Br. III, 312.

December 15, 1524. Luther to the Strassburg preachers. W. A., Br. III, 400-403; Walch XV:2047-2053.
October 30, 1525. Luther's Letter to Spalatin. W. A., Br. III, 593.

November 5, 1525. Luther's letter to Strassburg and instructions to Gregor Casel for the Strassburg preachers. W. A., Br. III, 599-612; Walch XVII:1533-1539.

Bibliographical Articles and Other Aids:

Bachmann, A. "Mittelhochdeutsches Lesebuch mit Grammatik und Wörterbuch". Zürich, 1964.

Die Religion in Geschichte und Gegenwart, 1956, Articles on "Bucer", "Karlstadt", "Abendmahl".

Dillenberger, John. "Luther Sudies, 1956-1959" *Church History*, vol. XXX, March 1961.

Encyclopedia Britannica, 1962 edition, vol. 22. Article on "Universities."

Erickson, A. "Über den handschriftlichen Nachlass und die gedruckten Briefe Butzers – Verzeichnis der Litterature über Butzer." *Zurjährigen Geburtsfeier Martrin Butzers*. Strassburg: J. H. Ed. Heitz, 1891. pp.165-180.

Götze, Alfred. "Frühneuhochdeutsches Glössar". Göttingen, 1920.

Grimm, Jakob und Wilhelm. "Deutsches Wörterbuch", 1854 ff.

Hertsch, Erich. "Karlstadts Schriften aus den Jahren 1523-25" Teil I, Halle (Salle), 1956.

Hubert, F. "Die Strassburger liturgischen Ordnungen im Zeitalter der Reformation", Göttingen, 1900.

Lilje, Hanns. "Luther and the Reformation, An Illustrated Review", Philadelphia, 1967.

Mentz, F. "Bibliographische Zusammenstellung der gedruckten Schriften Bucers", Strassburg, 1891.

Neue Deutsche Biographie. *Herausgegeben von der historischen Kommission bei der Bayerischen Akademie der Wissenschaften.* 5 volumes, Berlin, 1952-60.

Pauck, Wilhelm. "The Historiography of the German Reformation during the past 20 years", *Church History,* vol. IX, 1940, pp. 305-340.

Pollet, O. P. *Martin Bucer. Etudes sur la correspondence avec de nombreux textes inedits.* Vols. I and II. Paris, 1958 and 1962.

Richter, A. L. *Die evangelischen Kirchenordnungen des sechzehnten Jahrhunderts,* Vols, I and II, Weimar, 1846.

Schiess, Traugott. *Briefwechsel der Bruder Ambrosius und Thomas Blaurer, 1509-1548,* 3 volumes, G. Freiburg, 1908 ff.

Schottenlohrer, Karl. *Bibliographie zur deutschen Geschichte im Zeitalter der Glaubensspaltung, 1517-1585,* Volumes I – VI, second edition, Stuttgart, 1956-1958.

Sehling, Emil. *Die evangelischen Kirchenordnungen des XVI. Jahrhunderts,* Bd. I ff, Leipzig, 1902, 1904, 1909, 1911.

Stupperich, Robert. "Bibliographia Bucerana", *Schriften des Vereins für Reformationsgeschichte,* Nr. 169, Heft 2, Gütersloh, 1952.

Stupperich, Robert. "Forschungsbericht: Stand und Aufgabe der Butzer Forschung." *Archiv fur Reformationsgeschichte,* XLII, 1951, pp. 244-259.

Stupperich, Robert, ed. *Martini Buceri Opera Omnia, Deutsche Schriften,* Gütersloh, vol. I, 1960; vol. II, 1962.

Thompson, Bard. "Bucer Studies since 1918", *Church History,* vol. XXV, 1956, pp. 62-82.

Thompson, Bard. *Liturgies of the Western Church.* Cleveland & N.Y., 1961.

Secondary Sources

Adam, Johann. *Evangelische Kirchengeschichte der Stadt Strassburg.* Strassburg, 1922.

Aland, Kurt. *Martin Luther's 95 Theses.* Saint Louis, 1967.

Althaus, Paul. *The Theology of Martin Luther.* Philadelphia, 1966.

Anrich, Gustav. *Martin Bucer.* Strassburg, 1914.

Aulen, Gustaf. *Eucharist and Sacrifice.* Philadelphia, 1958.

Bainton, Roland E. *The Reformation of the Sixteenth Century.* Boston, 1952.

Barge, Hermann. *Andreas Bodenstein von Karlstadt. 2 vols.* Leipzig, 1905.

Baum, Adolf. *Magistrat und Reformation in Strassburg bis 1529.* Strassburg, 1887.

Baum, Johann W. *Capito und Butzer, Strassburgs Reformatoren.* Elberfeld, 1860.

Bizer, Ernst. *Studien zur Geschichte des Abendmahlstreits im 16. Jahrhundert.* Gutersloh, 1952.

Brown, Raymond E. *The Gospel of John.* New York, 1966.

Calvin, John. *Petit Traicte de la Sainte Cene.* Translated in the Library of Christian Classics, Vol. XXII, pp. 142-166. *(Short Treatise on the Holy Supper of our Lord and only Savior Jesus Christ).* Philadelphia, 1954.

Chrisman, Miriam Usher. *Strasbourg and the Reform.* Yale University Press, 1967.

Courvoisier, Jacques. *La notion d'eglise chez Bucer.* Strasbourg, 1933.

Courvoisier, Jacques. *Zwingli: A Reformed Theologian.* Richmond, Virginia, 1963.

Cypris, Ottomar F. *Public Worship in Calvin.* Unpublished dissertation, UTS

Library, New York, 1953.

Davies, Horton. *The Worship of the Puritans*. Westminster, 1948.

Douglas, E. Jane. *Justification in Late Medieval Preaching (Studies in Medieval and Reformation Thought: a study of John Geiler of Kaisersberg)*. Leiden, 1966.

Doumergue, Emil. *Essai sur l'histoire du culte reforme principalement au XVIe au XIXe siecle*. Paris, 1890.

Duffield, G. E. *The Works of Thomas Cranmer*. Philadelphia, 1965.

Duffield, G. E., ed. *John Calvin (Courtney Studies in Reformation Theology)*. Michigan, 1966.

Ebeling, Gerhard. *Luther: An Introduction to His Thought*. Philadelphia, 1970.

Eells, Hastings. *Martin Bucer*. New Haven, 1931.

Eells, Hastings. "The Genesis of Martin Bucer's Doctrine of the Lord's Supper". *Princeton Theological Review* XXIV, pp. 225-251, 1926.

Erichson, Alfred. *Martin Bucer*. Strassburg, 1951.

Gerbert, Camill. *Geschichte der Strassburger Sectenbewegung zur Zeit der Reformation*. Strassburg, 1889.

Grass, Hans. *Die Abendmahlslehre bei Luther und Calvin*. Gütersloh, 1954.

Green, V. H. H. *Renaissance and Reformation*. London, 1952.

Grimm, H. J. *The Reformation Era*. New York, 1954.

Harbison, E. Harris. *The Christian Scholar in the Age of the Reformation*. New York, 1956.

Heinisius, C. Maria. *Das unüberwindliche Wort: Frauen der Reformationszeit*. Munchen, 1951.

Hillerbrand, Hans J. *The Reformation,* New York, 1964.

Hillerbrand, Hans J. "Andreas Bodenstein von Karlstadt", pp. 379-398, *Church History*, Dec. 1966.

Hillerbrand, Hans J. *Men and Ideas in the Sixteenth Century*, Chicago, 1969.

Holborn, Hajo. *Ulrich von Hutten and the German Reformation*. New York, 1966.

Holborn, Hajo. *A History of Modern Germany: The Reformation*. New York, 1967.

Hopf, Constantin. *Martin Bucer and the English Reformation*. Oxford, 1946.

Huizinga, J. *The Waning of the Middle Ages*. London, 1948.

Jacoby, H. *Die Liturgik der Reformatoren: Vol. II: Die Litugik Melanchthons*. Gotha, 1876.

Jager, C. F. *Andreas Bodenstein von Carlstadt*. Stuttgart, 1856.

Jorgensen, Alfred Th. *Martin Luther, Reformer of the Church*. Minneapolis, 1953.

Kähler, Ernst. *Der Kommentar des Andreas Bodenstein von Karlstadt zu Augustins Schrift, 'De Spiritu et litera'*. Halle, 1952.

Koch, Karl. *Studium Pietatis: Martin Bucer als Ethiker*. Neukirchen, 1952.

Köhler, Walther. *Zwingli und Luther, ihr Streit über das Abendmahl nach seinen politischen und religiösen Beziehungen Vol. I, 1924, Vol. II*. Leipzig, 1958.

Köhler, Walther. *Das Marburger Religiongespräch 1529*. Tubingen, 1929.

Köhn, Mechtild. *Martin Bucers Entwurf einer Reformation des Erzstifts Köln*. Witten, 1966.

Kreider, Robert. "Anabaptists and the Civil Authorities of Strassburg", *Church History*, XXIV, pp.99-188.

Lang, August. *Der Evangelienkommentar Martin Butzers und die Grundzuge seiner Theologie*. Leipzig, 1900.

Lau, Franz. *Luther*. Philadelphia, 1963.

McDonnell, Killian. *John Calvin, the Church and the Eucharist*. Princeton, 1967.

McNeill, John T. *Unitive Protestantism*. Richmond, Virginia, 1964.

McNeill, John T. *The History and Character of Calvinism*. New York, 1967.

Manschreck, Clyde. *Melanchthon: The Quiet Reformer*. New York and Nashville, 1958.

Meyer, Boniface. "Calvin's Eucharistic Doctrine: 1536-39", *Journal of Ecumenical Studies*. Temple University, Philadelphia, 1969.

Niesel, Wilhelm. *Calvins Lehre vom Abendmahl*. München, 1930.

Obermann, Heiko A. *Forerunners of the Reformation*. New York, 1966.

Pannier, Jacques. *Calvin a Strasbourg*. Strasbourg, 1925.

Pauck, Wilhelm. *The Heritage of the Reformation*. Glencoe, Illinois, 1961.

Pauck, Wilhelm. *Melanchthon and Bucer*. Library of Christian Classics, Vol. XIX Philadelphia, 1969.

Pelikan, J. *Obedient Rebels*. New York, 1964.

Poll, G. J. Van De. *Martin Bucer's Liturgical Ideas: The Strasburg Reformer and his connection with the liturgies of the 16th century*. Assen, 1954.

Pollet, J. V., ed. *Martrin Bucer, etudes sur las correspondence*. 2 vols., Paris, 1959 and 1962.

Reed, Luther D. *The Lutheran Liturgy*. Philadelphia, 1947.

Richardson, C. C. *Zwingli and Cranmer on the Eucharist*. Evanston, 1949.

Rilliet, Jean. *Calvin, les temps et les destins*. Paris, 1963.

Rilliet, Jean. *Zwingli, Third Man of the Reformation*. Philadelphia, 1964.

Ritter, Gerhard. *Luther His Life and Work*. New York, 1963.

Ritschl, Otto. *Dogmengeschichte des Protestismus*. Göttingen, 1926.

Ritschl, Otto. *Reformation, Orthodoxie und Rationalismus*. Gütersloh, 1937.

Rupp, Gordon. *Patterns of Reformation*. Philadelphia, 1969.

Ritter, Gerhard. *Luther, His Life and Work*. New York, 1963.

Sasse, Herman. *This is My Body*. Minneapolis, 1959.

Schwiebert, E. G. *Luther and His Times*. St. Louis. 1950.

Seeberg, Emil. *Luthers Theologie in ihren Grundzugen*. Stuttgart, 1950.

Seeberg, Reinhold. *Lehrbuch der Dogmengeschichte*, IV, 1, 2 (6 Aufl.). Basel/Stuttgart, 1960.

Smend, Julius. *Die evangelischen deutschen Messen*. Göttingen, 1896.

Smend, Julius. *Der erst evangelische Gottesdienst in Strasburg*. Strasburg, 1897.

Stephens, W. P. *The Holy Spirit in the Theology of Martin Bucer*. Cambridge University Press, 1970.

Stupperich, Robert. *Martin Bucer. Der Reformator des Elassess und Einiger des deutschen Protestantismus*. Berlin, 1941.

Thiel, Rudolf. *Martin Luthers grosser Kampf ums Abendmahl*. München 1935.

Thompson, Bard. *Liturgies of the Western Church*. Cleveland and New York, 1961.

Todd, John M. *Martin Luther, a Biographical Study*. Newman Press, Maryland, 1965.

Torrance, T. F. *Kingdom and Church*. London, 1956.

Vatja, Vilmos. *Die Theologie des Gottesdienstes bei Luther*. Göttingen, 1952

(Abridged translation: *Luther on Worship*. Muhlenberg Press, Philadelphia, 1958).

Vatja, Vilmos, ed. *Luther and Melanchthon*. Philadelphia, 1961.

Wendel, Francois. *L'Eglise de Strasbourg, sa constitution et son organisation, 1532-35*. Paris, 1942.

Williams, George H. *The Radical Reformation*. Philadelphia, 1962.

Wunderli, Gustav. *Huldrych Zwingli und die Reformation in Zürich nach den Tagsatzungs-Protokollen*. Zürich, 1897.